Praise for *Better*

An important new exploration of mental fitness and how we can build a healthier mind, *Better* is for anyone interested in cultivating resilience, increasing well-being and reducing burnout.

—**Dean Mobbs,** professor of cognitive neuroscience and principal investigator of the Caltech Affect Lab

Better is a readable and compelling roadmap to mental fitness that takes the practice of self-compassion to another level.

—**Choden,** coauthor of *Mindful Compassion*

Better is a valuable distillation of behavioral science into simple, actionable rituals that protect our mental health and fuel our potential.

—**Kai Foong Tan,** organizational psychologist, executive coach and educator

Practical, punchy and deeply human, *Better* is the essential manual for anyone looking to master their mental fitness.

—**Vinod Kumar,** vice chairman of Everstone Group and CEO of Evercloud

Better is a thoughtful and accessible contribution to the field of mental fitness, inviting readers into deeper reflection, self-awareness and meaningful growth. Blending insight with practical application, it offers a culturally sensitive and human-centered approach that supports people to strengthen their inner world and create lasting change.

—**Clare Beckett-McInroy,** EdD, MCC, founder of BECKETT MCINROY and CoachME

Better is a rare guide that elevates our collective consciousness, reminding us that true performance begins with caring for our internal ecology. Aran Dadswell has written an essential book for every leader who understands that the most important infrastructure in any business is the mental fitness of its people.

—**Shifra Cook,** CEO of Ayda

What could be more important than to liberate ourselves from anxiety and guilt, and restore our personal power? In *Better*, Aran Dadswell unpacks practical, evidence-based practices, storytelling and reflective exercises to help build mental fitness for navigating our way through life's daily challenges. Dadswell brings an abundance of inspiring and simple strategies to cultivate clarity, strengthen resilience, enrich energy, and empower living with passion and purpose.

—**Linda Burks,** psychologist
and author of *Navigating Transitions*

Better is profoundly normalizing and helped me understand I'm not failing or falling behind—I am human. Fostering shifts with real-world consequences, this book offers a particularly valuable resource for people who feel capable yet disconnected.

—**Hazel E. Wallace,** social impact entrepreneur

Drawing on a lifetime of experience as a high-performance coach, Aran Dadswell has created this practical, energizing, well-researched book as an engaging guide to super-charging your own mental fitness.

—**Tiffany Wilding-White,** mental performance coach
and author of *Golfing with Your Eyes Closed*

Aran Dadswell's concept of mental fitness as a practical path to good mental health is a super helpful way to think about this complicated issue. She believes personal growth and wellbeing is a marathon, not a sprint. If you are looking for accessible mental fitness practices to help you train for your own personal growth marathon you will find them in *Better*. Sprinkled throughout are personal stories and humor to get your endorphins flowing as you read—an added bonus!

—**Beth Gibbs,** author of
Bitchcraft: Owning Your Power in a Complicated World

BETTER

Boost Your
Mental Fitness

BETTER

Boost Your Mental Fitness

ARAN DADSWELL

FOREWORD BY DR. DAVID WILKINSON AND SARAH SMITH
OF THE OXFORD REVIEW

EMERALD LAKE
BOOKS
Sherman, Connecticut

Better: Boost Your Mental Fitness

Books published by Emerald Lake Books may be ordered through your favorite booksellers or by visiting emeraldlakebooks.com.

Library of Congress Cataloging-in-Publication Data

Names: Dadswell, Aran, 1971- author
Title: Better : boost your mental fitness / Aran Dadswell.
Description: [Sherman, CT] : Emerald Lake Books, [2026] | Includes bibliographical references.
Identifiers: LCCN 2026007635 (print) | LCCN 2026007636 (ebook) | ISBN 9781945847929 paperback | ISBN 9781945847943 | ISBN 9781945847936 epub
Subjects: LCSH: Mental health promotion | Mental health--Philosophy | Self-care, Health | Resilience (Personality trait) | LCGFT: Self-help publications
Classification: LCC RA790.53 .D34 2026 (print) | LCC RA790.53 (ebook) | DDC 616.890082--dc23/eng/20260424
LC record available at https://lccn.loc.gov/2026007635
LC ebook record available at https://lccn.loc.gov/2026007636

To my darling Wiremu and princess Yasmin, you make my life better.

To Sara, Michael and Andy, so do you.

Table of Contents

Foreword

We have both known Aran Dadswell for some years now, through her quiet but persistent presence in the Oxford Review's research community. She is the kind of member every editor hopes for: thoughtful, generous, genuinely interested in what the evidence has to say, and with a way of asking better questions than most. *Better* reads like the book she has been preparing, patiently and seriously, to write for a very long time.

In the years I have spent reviewing research on leadership, learning and human flourishing, I have read more wellbeing books than I care to admit. Most fall into one of two camps. Some assemble a handful of studies, decorate them with anecdotes, and present a tidy formula for happiness. Others reach for the spiritual and the inspirational without much patience for the awkward, contradictory texture of how human beings actually live. Both can be useful. Neither tends to wear well.

Better is something different.

The first thing to say about it is that the book knows what it is, and what it is not. It does not promise transformation. It does not insist that everything is awesome. It does not flatten the messiness of being human into a sequence of confident steps. What it offers instead is a framework, five cornerstones of togetherness, meaning, resourcefulness, resilience and wellbeing, and forty-two practical "boosters" (plus a ten-stage rocket booster) the reader is invited to try, adapt or set aside. The framing is deliberate. As Aran writes, the title is *Better*, not *best*; the project is gentler, more honest and, for that, more useful.

The second thing to say is that this is an unusually well-read book. Aran draws on Brené Brown and Sarah-Jayne Blakemore, on Owen Eastwood and Wade Davis, on contemplative traditions and contemporary cognitive science, flattening none of them. She treats her sources as scaffolding rather than ornament. There is no shortage of mental fitness content in the world. Very little of it is grounded with this much care.

The third thing, and for us the most important, is the tone. Aran is candid about the fact that she, too, has shitty days. She does not present herself as someone who has solved being human. The whole book proceeds from the reasonable assumption that suffering is part of the territory and that the work is not to eliminate it but to meet it more skillfully. That posture, self-compassion without self-indulgence, is rarer in this literature than it ought to be, and it is wholly characteristic of the Aran we know.

It also reflects a particular kind of credibility. After close to two decades in corporate roles, Aran turned her attention to people, earning a master's in mindfulness studies, a diploma in learning and development, and a Master Certified Coach credential with the International Coaching Federation. She is, in short, someone who has done the work and who is unusually attentive to the difference between an idea that holds up and one that merely sounds good. The boosters in this book bear that out.

Much of our own work sits with management consultants, organizational leaders, and learning professionals, thinking about the conditions under which people and teams do good work under pressure. The themes of *Better* will feel familiar to anyone in those fields: psychological safety, regulation under load, the relationship between meaning and motivation, the quiet power of belonging. What this book adds is a way of bringing those ideas back to the level at which they ultimately have to live: the level of the individual, on a Tuesday morning, doing their best while the world keeps moving.

The questions Aran asks here—How do I look after my mind? How do I stay connected? How do I keep going when things are hard?—are not new. But in an age of accelerating change, eroding attention, and considerable uncertainty about what work and meaning will look like in the years ahead, the case for cultivating mental fitness, deliberately and patiently, has rarely been more pressing.

You do not need to agree with every page to benefit from this guide. I am sure Aran would not want you to. Take what works, leave the rest, return when you are ready. That is, after all, the point of the book.

We commend it to you warmly.

Dr. David Wilkinson and Sarah Smith
The Oxford Review

Better, Not Best

Approximately two and a half hours south of Auckland, New Zealand, lies an extraordinary place called Waitomo Caves, an extensive cave system discovered in the late nineteenth century. It is a renowned tourist destination, and people come from all over the world to visit. The most popular excursion begins with an enchanting walk through vast chambers filled with limestone formations before taking a boat ride through underground grottos to silently observe thousands of glowworms illuminating the ceiling like a starry sky.

A world away from this captivating location is the driest place on earth: the Atacama Desert in northern Chile. After the sun sets, as the temperature plummets, a mesmerizing blanket of stars becomes visible in every direction, stretching all the way to the horizon.

For most people, these two majestic locations offer magical, memorable experiences. But not always. A silent boat ride, where any loud noise can scare the glowworms into hiding, can feel like a nightmare for a sleep-deprived parent desperately trying to console a cute yet highly volatile toddler on the brink of a meltdown. And a star-studded desert sky is not so enchanting if your rental car has a flat tire, your water bottle is empty, your phone battery has died, and you feel as if you're in the middle of nowhere—a notion reinforced by a landscape that looks suspiciously like the moon.

Context means everything. It can make the difference between a person being able to meet the challenges that come their way with composure and resilience or sinking under their weight.

We are all the same, but different. And we are constantly changing from moment to moment, as is the context of our lived experience. Maintaining our mental health, whatever the circumstances, can be difficult, and yet doing so is critical to achieving contentment and fulfillment in our time here on earth.

Having a framework for mental fitness is valuable for you as an individual and for humanity. The challenge is to ensure its structure is flexible enough to offer value regardless of context or change, which is kind of like having a one-size-fits-all glass slipper for Cinderella. As Sarah-Jayne Blakemore remarks in *Inventing Ourselves* (a must-read for every parent), "Individual differences are lost in stereotypes." That is why the heart and soul of this book firmly upholds a you-do-you approach.

The mental fitness framework I present here is intended to be both validated and verified by the transformation you experience through applying what you learn. I hope it is valuable to you as an individual while simultaneously contributing toward a positive outcome for everyone else.

I've intentionally chosen the title *Better* for this book. It's not about becoming the "best," which can manifest paralyzing expectations. The healthier alternative term, "better," serves as a guide, empowering you with autonomy to decipher what that might mean for you. This approach is a warm, compassionate tribute to growth. As you work through the book's content, you will discern what's useful and interesting to you, and discard what's not. These are situationally driven decisions that only you can make. As Héctor García and Francesc Miralles say in their book *Ikigai,* "Life is not a problem to be solved. Just remember to have something that keeps you busy doing what you love while being surrounded by the people who love you."

The strength of your mental fitness depends largely on your awareness and understanding of what it is and how it works, which increases your ability to improve, harness or magnify it. Mental fitness is optimistic and forgiving; if things don't work so well today, there's always hope for a better tomorrow.

As You Get Started

THROUGHOUT THIS BOOK, I talk about your "bounce score," which is a snapshot of the current state of your mental fitness. This will fluctuate over time, maybe even throughout the day. Tracking your bounce score draws your attention to aspects of your mental fitness, and you can determine whether you need or want to do anything with that information. It might be hugely interesting and useful to calculate your score as you begin reading this book and again after you're done to make a comparison. (I will explain how to do this in Chapter 1.)

There's something crucial about mental fitness that I want to cover right up front: It requires having self-compassion. Let me paint a picture for you that shows you want I mean.

Unless you were stranded in the Atacama Desert and subsequently lived in an old, abandoned mining town for years, you've likely heard of Catherine, Princess of Wales, more commonly referred to as Princess Kate.

When you think of her, what comes to mind? Perhaps it's her natural beauty, elegance and radiant smile. Or maybe it's her remarkable journey from university student to future queen, philanthropist and mother to heirs to the throne. Now consider some of the challenging aspects of her life. Do you think about her battle with cancer, how she's constantly judged on her physical appearance, or the lack of autonomy she undoubtedly experiences due to living as a public figure? Whatever thoughts just crossed your mind, it's entirely probable that they naturally evoked your sense of empathy, sympathy or both.

Here's the thing: If you can so easily feel this way regarding a stunningly gorgeous princess, why is it so hard to feel sad or sorry for yourself when it's *you* who is suffering, for whatever reason? Why is it that you can dismiss your distress so readily, or even worse, allow it to envelop you in layers of guilt or shame?

Suffering is part of the human condition. It will always be that way. No one escapes from it, and no amount of effort we make will eliminate it. We can only aspire to ease our pain, and this guide is designed with that in mind.

Please be kind to yourself on this journey by avoiding unrealistic expectations. "Everything is awesome" fits as a cool mantra for *The Lego Movie*, but not as a lived, human experience.

I focus on mental fitness personally and professionally every single day, and I still have shitty days. So will you. The intention of this guide is to help you regulate and moderate better during these periods of time. I hope you can accept that and gently give yourself permission to suffer. By suffering, I mean feeling emotions like anger or experiencing low self-confidence or anxiety. As Ruby Wax, the legendary comedian and mental health advocate, points out, "It's okay to not be okay." And in the twenty-first century, it's becoming apparent that the negative effects of suppressing or ignoring our feelings are exponentially greater than if we all just admit we're not immune to suffering, nor do we have any control over it, as much as we might like to.

Using This Guide

This book consists of three parts.

1. **Part One** provides context and is an exploration of the past, present and future of mental fitness as a concept.

2. **Part Two** defines the Better Mental Fitness Framework, introducing in detail the five cornerstones of togetherness, meaning, resourcefulness, resilience and wellbeing.
3. **Part Three** offers the practical elements needed to help you nourish, cultivate and nurture your mental fitness. These "boosters" are categorized in such a way that you can quickly and easily locate one that matches your needs and that makes the material as accessible as possible.

Boosters are techniques, tools or tips that may be useful mental fitness practices for you. The ones I offer here range from quick and easy options to others that require more time and focus. I've provided forty-two, plus a ten-stage Mental Fitness Rocket Booster, so you can try a new practice every week over the course of a year. Or, if you want to fast-track your adventure, perhaps try four per week over a season (for example, spring, summer, fall or winter). Decide on the most suitable cadence for your needs and experiment with them.

I highly recommend repeating each booster at least once since some might grow on you with practice. Each one has been designed—or molded if it's derived from another technique—for broad applicability and to be effective across various contexts and situations.

I have created a tracker you can use to record your experiences, preferences and reflections, which you can download at mentalfitnessforhumans.com/tracker.

My three hopes for you, as you journey through *Better*, are that:

1. you find a few boosters that truly resonate and remain with you for a long time.
2. this guide awakens or affirms your belief in your capacity to take steps proactively to boost your mental fitness, by you, for you.

3. whatever you glean from this guide enables you to achieve ongoing contentment and fulfillment in your life.

Remember, mental fitness is personal; what works wonders for you might not appeal to someone else, and even your own experience can vary from day to day. I hope you discover the boosters that work brilliantly for you.

Part One:
Exploring Mental Fitness

Chapter 1
Rethinking Mental Fitness

Mental fitness is how you navigate through life. It consists of five cornerstones of human experience (togetherness, meaning, resourcefulness, resilience and wellbeing) that, when nourished, may prevent mental health deterioration or, better yet, increase contentment and fulfillment. Who doesn't want or need that amid the uncertainty and complexity of modern-day living? These cornerstones form the Better Mental Fitness Framework introduced in this book. Developing these foundational elements is a means to an end. Similar to how cardio and strength training contribute to your physical health, maintaining and improving mental fitness positively affects one's sense of contentment and fulfillment in life.

The intention is not to unveil "the mystery of how something as sublime and insubstantial as thought or consciousness can emerge from three pounds of gelatinous pudding inside the skull," as so delightfully articulated by Jeffrey Schwartz and Sharon Begley in their book *The Mind and the Brain*. Nor is it to dictate or specify what needs to be addressed by an individual to develop mental fitness through a formulaic instruction manual for human improvement. The aim is to reveal what lives within each of us: to recognize the abundance of our nature and what is yet to be explored.

Balance supports mental fitness as its indispensable foundation, facilitating the interplay *of* and the equilibrium *within* the five cornerstones, which are of equal significance. As you journey through this book, you'll determine how to achieve an optimal balance for you, with increasing personal contentment and fulfillment at the heart of your efforts.

To understand mental fitness more deeply, let's explore it from a few perspectives, including its dynamic nature and how it relates to happiness and motivation. Then, we will delve into the concept of "bounce" and how it ties into the Better Mental Fitness Framework.

The Dynamic Nature of Mental Fitness

One of the most complicated aspects of mental fitness is its fluidity and dynamism. It is continually changing, much like the ocean. We may be able to break it down into parts we can study and understand—such as its tides, temperatures and ecosystems—but it still remains unpredictable and vast.

Have you ever walked along the beach after a storm? There's so much flotsam and jetsam to look at, dredged up by turbulent waters. (Wow! I never imagined I would actually use those words, but there they are.) Some things may be mesmerizing and magical, like perfect shiny pāua shells (the Māori word for abalone), while others are downright stinky and gross. Similarly, practicing mental fitness requires constant attention to keep up with the endless possibilities that change creates, no matter what surfaces from the depths.

I'm quick to acknowledge that I'm incredibly fortunate to be living and breathing mental fitness through my work, and I see its impact on all aspects of my life. However, the majority of your time, energy, attention and money are probably spent on a wide range of other things. It is enormously beneficial to attend to your mental fitness intentionally as often as you need, to embed the concept into your thinking and weave its practices into your behavior until they're second nature.

Just as winter may bring a blizzard or summer a heatwave, you will navigate through harsh, bitter seasons as well as sunny, temperate ones. Isn't it astounding how changeable you are from moment to moment, with a complex internal world that exists alongside a complicated external one?

Before you wake up each day, plenty has already happened to and beyond you that influences your journey. We are made up of systems within systems, and nothing ever happens in isolation. Individually and collectively, mental fitness shapes our lived experience, which in turn affects our mental fitness.

Mental Fitness and Happiness

Mental fitness doesn't equate to being happy. A quote often attributed to Mahatma Gandhi says, "Happiness is when what you think, what you say, and what you do are in harmony." But how consistently can we achieve this harmony, and how do we measure it—in moments or over a longer period? Paradoxically, a constant pursuit of happiness can lead to dissatisfaction. As Toby Qin, one of the most talented technologists I've ever had the pleasure of coaching, asserts, "There's no path to happiness. Happiness is the path."

I use the word *happiness* with caution. As a concept, I think it's jam-packed with pressure and the futile pursuit of perfection. In a complicated world with a constant backdrop of serious issues—including the cost of living, unemployment, poverty, social inequalities, crime, climate and war—moments of feeling happy are fabulous, but fleeting. Happiness offers hedonistic highs, yet fortunately, humanity has developed a far more sophisticated palate for contentment and fulfillment.

That being said, happiness and mental fitness influence one another, but they're not the same thing, which we'll explore more later in the book.

Mental Fitness and Motivation

If we trace the forces behind our experiences back to their core, many seem to arise from two basic motivations: fear and love. How does this massive oversimplification align with our mental fitness? When we correlate it to the science of approach and avoidance motivation, popularized by Andrew Elliott, these factors are the driving push and pull of our existence.

Thousands of years ago, these motivational factors equated to survival and reproduction—the primal struggle of avoiding the jaws and claws of predators while simultaneously ensuring species evolution. Now, in the twenty-first century, most of us have the luxury, privilege and autonomy of living our lives to achieve far more. We're not merely reacting to immediate threats or driven solely by biological imperatives. Fear and love have become the roots of an existential tree that has grown branches and leaves in every direction.

We now seek purpose, connection and transcendence. It is fortuitous that we can ask ourselves truly meaningful questions. We craft cathedrals and skyscrapers, compose symphonies and rap songs, explore the depths of oceans and the breadth of the cosmos, and push the boundaries of human potential on the sports field and the track. The expansiveness of the love we experience seems to know no bounds, encompassing people, animals, experiences and objects. We love through memory, in the present and with hope for the future, defying the limitations of time.

For the lucky people, love is a key motivational factor, compelling them to bounce out of bed every day. Mental fitness and motivation are in full alignment as complementary concepts.

The Concept of Bounce

Bounce is a word with multiple definitions, one of which describes it as a type of rhythm or energy. This does a pretty good job of offering a context for how to understand mental fitness. At the beginning of the millennium, a popular sports show called *Soccer AM* aired on UK television on Saturday mornings. Presenters Helen Chamberlain and Tim Lovejoy fronted a super enjoyable and funny campaign around a made-up word, "bouncebackability." They were on a mission to popularize this term that was coined by the then-manager of Crystal Palace, Iain Dowie, enough to have it recognized as an official entry in the English dictionary. They encouraged pundits and players to use it, and viewers waited with bated breath to hear it during broadcasted UK football interviews. Bouncebackability is such a perfect description of resilience that when I discovered Diane Coutu's work "How Resilience Works: Three Traits of Those Who Bounce Back," I almost cried tears of joy and delight when I read the subtitle!

According to Dan Siegel, founder of the Mindsight Institute, all human interactions involve the transfer of information and energy. It is easy to understand what it means when we think about sharing information. But what does it mean to send and receive energy?

We are, at our essence, energy personified. This is true whether you view it through a scientific or spiritual worldview, which makes the concept of "bounce" highly relevant to mental fitness. At their core, our interactions with the outer world and the way our inner world functions are expressions of how we manage, regulate and move that energy.

It can be helpful to think of the five cornerstones of mental fitness in relation to bounce:

1. **Togetherness:** Bounce with
2. **Meaning:** Bounce for
3. **Resourcefulness:** Bounce through
4. **Resilience**: Bounce back
5. **Wellbeing:** Bounce well

Your bounce score is a snapshot of your satisfaction in each of these categories, offering insight into your mental fitness. This enables you to understand it and, more importantly, identify what you need to nurture at any given moment. At various points throughout this book, you will be invited to calculate your scores. This is based on a quick self-assessment of how you are doing in relation to each of the cornerstones of mental fitness.

On a scale of 1 (low) to 10 (high), rate how you are doing *today* in each of these areas:

9-10 = Phenomenal
8 = Flourishing
6-7 = Doing well
5 = Hmm
3-4 = Uh-oh
1-2 = Oh sh*t

1. **Bounce With:** How would you rate your sense of belonging and connection to others?
2. **Bounce For:** How would you rate your sense of life's meaning, purpose and overall significance?
3. **Bounce Through:** How would you rate your ability to think clearly, feel empowered, and take effective action?
4. **Bounce Back:** How would you rate your ability to navigate through and recover from adversity, challenges and setbacks?
5. **Bounce Well:** How would you rate your sense of inner harmony, vitality and life satisfaction?

The next time you rate yourself on a given cornerstone, it allows you to compare where you were with how far you have come and what work is yet to be done. If you prefer simplicity and would like to have just one bounce score for your overall mental fitness, then go for it! In that case, anything over 30 puts you in the "Doing well" camp.

By understanding the source, essence and practical applications of these mental fitness cornerstones, we harness the opportunity to ease our suffering, harvest contentment and fulfillment, and restore balance. Every day, we can give ourselves another chance to feel, think and be better.

Chapter 2
Mainstreaming Mental Fitness

While the work of renowned 19th-century psychologist William James provided a blueprint for "mental fitness," I am sometimes met with a vacant stare when I tell people I am a "mental fitness coach." Although "mental health" garnered warranted attention in the last century, mental fitness has remained largely out of the spotlight. One possible cause is the lack of a clear framework surrounding it. When people aren't familiar with an expression, they'll often refrain from using it to avoid getting it wrong—especially when a similar sounding phrase like "mentally unfit" carries an altogether different meaning. As a result, while terms like mental health and physical fitness easily roll off the tongue, mental fitness remains relatively uncommon, despite not being new at all.

However, as Harvard's Ellen Langer puts it in her book *Mindfulness*, "we are in the midst of a revolution in consciousness." In August 2024, a Google search for the phrase "mental fitness" delivered about 18,800 results in 0.06 seconds. In June 2025, the same query yielded about 1,260,000,000 results in 0.24 seconds. I'm no mathematical genius, but that seems like a staggering increase in ten months, even accounting for changes to algorithms. My Spidey senses tell me we're on the cusp of mental fitness becoming "a thing," much like other terms, such as wellbeing, self-care and mindfulness, which have gained widespread acceptance and developed as mainstream concepts since the turn of the century. It appears our progress toward contentment and fulfillment is gaining momentum.

In Bonnie Garmus's astoundingly good, bestselling novel *Lessons in Chemistry*, set in the 1950s and '60s, one of her characters, the brilliant, unconventional scientist Calvin Evans, is a jogger. Back then, recreational jogging was a weird thing to do. In fact, it was practically nonexistent as a fitness activity until a progressive and innovative Kiwi named Arthur Lydiard, lovingly known as the "Father of Jogging," changed that.

In 1961, Lydiard established the Auckland Jogging Club in New Zealand, believed to be the world's first club specifically for recreational runners. This was a revolutionary concept. In the early 1960s, American track coach Bill Bowerman (later the cofounder of Nike) visited Arthur. Inspired by Arthur's ideas and his notable success as a coach at the 1960 Olympics in Rome, as well as the sight of ordinary people running along suburban streets for fitness, Bill returned to the US and, with cardiologist Waldo E. Harris, coauthored the book *Jogging*, published in 1967. This guide became a bestseller and was a primary catalyst for the fitness boom in North America, and subsequently, globally.

Okay, *Better*, now it's time to mainstream mental fitness! Arthur, Bill and Waldo's straightforward advocacy for running as a universal activity for health paved the way. It's time to shine the spotlight on what you can do for mental health.

In *The Art of Happiness*, the Dalai Lama states:

> I believe that the very purpose of our life is to seek happiness. That is clear. Whether one believes in religion or not, whether one believes in this religion or that religion, we all are seeking something better in life. So, I think, the very motion of our life is toward happiness...

While I may not be a big fan of the word *happiness*, I still love this sentiment. It may be more helpful, though, to think in terms of "happy moments," which acknowledges that happiness is temporary and removes the pressure to feel it all the time. Focusing on creating more of these moments is a far more achievable aim—and one that can genuinely increase our sense of contentment and fulfillment.

Mental Fitness in the 21st Century

The shift from seeking an abstract goal to practicing a tangible skill is precisely why we are seeing a global movement unfold. In 2025, as a positive counterpart to World Mental Health Day (celebrated on October 10), a handful of people acknowledged the inaugural World Mental Fitness Day on April 10. Everything starts somewhere, and often something has been brewing for years before it's regarded as "an overnight success."

Let's unpack that for a second. At the start of the twenty-first century, if you had stopped someone on the street and asked whether they had a coach, they'd probably have assumed you'd mistaken them for an athlete. Few people had ever heard of a leadership, executive or life coach. However, I believe that by 2035, or even sooner, *mental fitness* will have earned its place in everyday language, becoming the phrase we use to describe how we navigate through life and care for our rich and individual inner worlds. The Better Mental Fitness Framework provides a simple structure to aid in achieving that goal.

By engaging with the insights and practices in this book, you are actively choosing to train your mind, contributing to this revolution in consciousness and helping to mainstream mental fitness for yourself and for humanity.

The "B" Word: Burnout

"Burnout" is tossed around almost too frequently these days, often used to describe anything from being a bit tired to feeling utterly fed up. Back in my early 30s, I returned to work after a miscarriage, and my boss brazenly exclaimed he was so tired it was like he had had a miscarriage too! It drives me nuts when people make careless comparisons like that, which is downright disrespectful and dismissive. Burnout is a serious issue, a warning light flashing on your internal dashboard, indicating something has malfunctioned and is chipping away at, or is even destroying, your mental health.

Burnout is not simply about feeling exhausted or irritated after a long day. It is a complex syndrome—a psychophysiological state brought on by chronic workplace stress that hasn't been successfully managed. And here's a whopper: The World Health Organization (WHO) officially recognized it as an occupational phenomenon in the *International Classification of Diseases (ICD-11)*, 11th Revision, adopted in May 2019, long before the global COVID-19 pandemic took hold.

While the way it's sometimes used implies otherwise, this isn't just a casual term. It's a formal acknowledgment that burnout is primarily a work-related issue, and most definitely not a personal failing. Think of it like this: Your body and mind are sophisticated systems, designed to handle stress, but only up to a point. When it becomes chronic, relentless and unmanaged, things start to break down. We see this play out in three key dimensions: emotional exhaustion, depersonalization (or cynicism), and reduced personal accomplishment.

Emotional exhaustion isn't just a bit of tiredness; it's a deep-seated depletion of resources. Neurobiologically, chronic stress can dysregulate your hypothalamic-pituitary-adrenal axis and disrupt normal cortisol patterns, which is associated with changes in brain regions involved in mood and cognition and can contribute to sleep disturbances, appetite changes, and mood swings. It's like your emotional battery is running on fumes, and while you might be able to keep going in a tired but wired state for a while, you can't run on empty forever.

Then there's depersonalization, that detached, cynical feeling. You view your work and colleagues through a negative lens, distancing yourself emotionally. This can be linked to changes in your prefrontal cortex, affecting your cognitive control and emotional processing. It's harder to inhibit your negative behaviors, understand information as quickly as you're used to, remember things, and make better decisions.

And finally, there's a reduced sense of personal accomplishment, and the feeling that what you do is meaningless and that you're ineffective. This isn't just a bad day; there's a persistent undercurrent of inefficacy, often tied to a perceived lack of control and autonomy in your work environment. You know how capable you are, and that you'd still be full of potential in the right setting, and yet you can also observe you aren't performing to your own standards at the moment. That makes you feel even worse about yourself, so the downward spiral perpetuates itself.

From a physiological perspective, chronic stress leads to prolonged activation of your sympathetic nervous system, flooding your body with adrenaline and noradrenaline. This can contribute to cardiovascular issues, immune system dysfunction, and cognitive impairments. Your entire autonomic nervous system, comprised of both the sympathetic and parasympathetic systems, gets thrown out of balance, making it harder for you to recover. This creates another downward spiral, leaving you in a state of constant arousal or, as prominent neuropsychiatry expert John Ratey aptly describes it in *A User's Guide to the Brain*, "hyped up."

Stress-related illnesses can have a profound effect on everything. According to the WHO, work-related stress contributes to:

1. millions of deaths annually from cardiovascular and other stress-related diseases.
2. significant economic losses due to both absenteeism and presenteeism (in other words, reduced productivity).
3. increased risk of mental health conditions, such as depression and anxiety.
4. a substantial burden on healthcare systems.

If you're reading this and contemplating whether you might be experiencing burnout, take a moment to reflect on the past few months. Have you noticed a persistent decline in your energy, motivation or overall wellbeing? Is there a growing sense of cynicism or detachment from your work? Now, calculate the date three months ago. Do you think you were feeling this way and experiencing these symptoms back then? How about six months ago? Has it been even longer than that?

Recognizing patterns is a crucial first step in addressing burnout and reclaiming your mental fitness. If it's becoming apparent to you that you are suffering from burnout, know you're not alone and, importantly, that you may also need support in dealing with this serious issue with resources other than just this book. Therefore, take the time to work out who you might speak with and get the help you deserve.

You may be asking yourself: *Is it burnout or something else?* If you're unsure, talk to someone. Find either a health professional or other person you can trust (a) not to dismiss what is concerning you, (b) not to make the conversation all about them and how they are most definitely suffering from burnout, and (c) not to shove their head in the sand and stick to superficial conversations, like what to binge-watch next. There are sure to be people in your life who hinder more than help, regardless of how well-meaning they might be or how much they love and care for you. If you already know who has a tendency to drive you nuts, dodge this conversation with them and select someone else to have it with.

And another thing... Can we stop pretending that burnout only happens to those who are working sixty-hour weeks? Burnout doesn't discriminate. It can affect you just as severely if you're working part-time, volunteering or in any other scenario. In fact, I would propose that specifying the "workplace" as a condition for burnout is too limiting since being involved in any type of organization can be toxic, and it's highly contextualized by relationships with other people. The WHO acknowledges burnout is an "occupational" phenomenon. A common definition of *occupation* in a professional context is "a person's regular work, job, profession or principal activity by which they earn a living." However, a broader meaning proposes that it is defined as "any activity in which a person is engaged or spends their time."

When we contemplate these perspectives on burnout, the far-reaching positive impact of mental fitness becomes abundantly clear. Timeless wisdom is offered in the powerful progression described by William James: "Sow an action, reap a habit; sow a habit, reap a character; sow a character, reap a destiny."

By mainstreaming mental fitness, we can empower individuals jogging along a journey of personal development with a practical way to find greater contentment and fulfillment. One might think of mental fitness as being running shoes for the mind.

Chapter 3
Prioritizing Mental Fitness

Who is the most important person in the universe? Of course, it's *you*. While it is simultaneously every. single. other. individual on the planet, it's also undeniably, and most definitely, you.

The exquisite words of Björn Natthiko Lindeblad, from his book *I May Be Wrong*, capture the significance of prioritizing mental fitness:

> We don't live in a random, indifferent universe. Quite the opposite. There's a resonance in this existence. The universe responds to the intentions behind what we do and say. What we send out eventually comes back. The world is not as it is. The world is as *you* are. So be what you want to see in it.

When the COVID pandemic hit, the phrase "put your own oxygen mask on first" resurfaced, which conveys the importance of self-care. How unfortunate, then, that an underlying sense of guilt and shame often hinders us from practicing it, despite the benefits to ourselves, our loved ones, our communities, and society as a whole.

Perhaps that guilt stems from the Industrial Revolution, which prioritized productivity above all else. Or maybe it was drummed into us as kids not to be selfish and to think of others first, or perhaps we heard another similar narrative that conveyed how awful we were for taking care of our own needs when we should have been winning, working and not whining. In many respects, prioritizing mental fitness is easier said than done.

Becoming Your Own Responsible Agent

If you're not used to being the "main character" in the game of your life, it may require unlearning old habits and thinking patterns before you can make visible progress. It's a pretty hefty ask of you to take on this responsibility. And despite how it may sound on a superficial level, it has nothing to do with prioritizing oneself over others. As former Buddhist nun Martine Batchelor puts it in her book *Let Go*:

> We have a choice. Do we want change to be the result of a chaotic breakdown, or do we want to be a responsible agent, creatively involved in the flux and transformation of our own lives?

What could be more important to you and everyone else than prioritizing mental fitness centered on togetherness, meaning, resourcefulness, resilience and wellbeing? You are worthy of experiencing as much contentment and fulfillment in your life as is possible given your circumstances. When you do, you embody the very definition of conscious effort that meditation pioneer Jon Kabat-Zinn uses to describe practicing mindfulness. You are "taking responsibility for being yourself and learning to listen to and trust your own being."

I've worked with plenty of clients who identify as people-pleasers and who struggle with this shift, despite it making total sense to them. If it's too ghastly to contemplate prioritizing your mental fitness for your own sake in this chapter of your life, then do it for everyone else. You can thank us all later. Prioritization is about effectively evaluating tasks, goals and activities to focus and maximize effort. If you become aware of how aligned your behavior is with your mental fitness, then you will also recognize any misalignment you ought to address.

The intention is to prioritize mental fitness to feel better. Whether that means you are optimizing it, addressing burnout, or both, "better" in this context implies growth and advancement rather than striving for perfection, which can be detrimental and potentially undermine efforts to improve mental fitness. Remain focused on progress, not unrealistic ideals.

Challenging Your Inner Voices

Rob Nairn was a well-regarded and beloved pioneer of Buddhist and Western mindfulness. In his book, *Diamond Mind*, he wrote:

> In our culture, people who are insane are said to have unstable minds, but actually, all our minds are unstable. They are unstable in the sense that powerful mental and emotional states can overwhelm us when they arise, and throw the mind off balance. That's instability—the fact that we are susceptible to being thrown off balance.

He spoke of the three arrows of suffering. The first arrow is whatever has caused the suffering to begin with, such as having an argument with a loved one or tripping and twisting your ankle. It is an event that has taken place in a moment of time. Next comes the second arrow: your interpretation of what has taken place. This is where things can turn negative, since we so often heap a whole lot of guilt, shame, anger or embarrassment on top of what happened. The third arrow adds insult to injury by dolloping on some nastiness, with scathing thoughts like, *Something's completely screwed up with me if I'm reacting so badly.*

Sound familiar? The number of times I've shared this idea with people has been met with an equal number of relieved sighs that these toxic narratives are common. And yet it is *so* hard to spot this pattern when it's happening, let alone prevent it in the first place.

If we don't challenge this self-cruelty, you can imagine how quickly it consumes us. Infections, weeds and wildfires spread rapidly in favorable conditions, as do our negative internal narratives. No wonder there's a mental health crisis raging if we're not putting a stop to this meanness. Remember, *easing* suffering over *ceasing* suffering; that is our quest.

As you're reading this, is there a small voice in your head that's being a contemptuous little arse? Telling you things like "You're not worthy of self-care" or "You're so self-centered! It's pathetic to be contemplating yourself in the role of the main character!"

What if you applied the idea of a daily wellness routine—like eating your five servings of fruit and vegetables—to your mental fitness? If you're lucky enough to have two hands, each with five fingers, then you can use the other hand to count sleep, hydration, nutrition, exercise and mental fitness as your daily essentials. That spells SHNEMF! (Gesundheit!)

If you're convinced by now and have resolved to act immediately to prioritize your mental fitness—and encourage the people near or dear to you to do the same—you're ready to move on to the next chapter of this book. Or maybe you need a bit more encouragement because those inner voices are relentless. They bleat at you like hungry little lambs, but are much less cute and way more savage.

The point is—you're not alone in grappling with thoughts that are unkind, toxic and nasty. In fact, one of the titles I contemplated for this book was *You're Crazy, Just Like Me*

(Said Eight Billion People)! I wake up every single day and have to begin anew to address my grumpy, whiny inner voices. Simply wishing away what surfaces is futile and draining. Yet self-compassion, curiosity and emotion regulation help me counteract the shadows.

If you don't weed, the flowers cannot grow. If you don't allow your body to heal from an infection, it will take longer to recover. If you don't maintain firebreaks, wildfire will obliterate a forest. And if you don't prioritize mental fitness, your mental health will suffer.

Imagine all the time, energy, attention and money that could be saved by cultivating your mental fitness. What ripple effect might this have on your loved ones, your community and beyond?

The Era of Impatience

If you're anywhere near as old as I am, you might recall your childhood being filled with desire and anticipation. At that point in your life, you likely had zero trouble placing yourself at the center of the universe. If you grew up before online shopping was as natural as breathing, then you can probably remember a birthday or other gift-giving celebration when you were desperate for something; a Barbie doll, a bike, your favorite artist's newest album, Nintendo Octopus, skates, Lego, Pac-Man... You get my drift. Patience was an essential trait, and instant gratification only happened in the movies.

As a kid growing up in a small town in New Zealand, I got my first after-school job when I was eight. I can't quite remember how old I was when "all I ever wanted" was a Healing 10 Speed bike, just like my big sister's cool green one. But when I had finally saved up $110, off I went with Mum to John Kidd's Cycles and Mowers shop to celebrate my purchase: not exactly the make and model I had coveted, but a glorious shiny blue

Morrison Freeway. Mum followed behind in the car as I rode home, beaming.

In the twenty-first century, the time lag between deciding to read this book and obtaining a copy in your preferred format, whether that be print, digital or audio, is minimal. Wait times have been obliterated, and near-instant gratification is the norm. It still astounds me that I can move so swiftly from realizing a want or need to having the thing in my hot little hands.

Where I live now in the UK, the luxury of same-day delivery often means I can think of something in the morning and have my dear friend Amazon Prime deliver it to my door by 10 p.m. This starkly contrasted with a trip home to New Zealand for Christmas in 2024, where I was genuinely shocked. One online order from a major retailer took nine days just to be ready for in-store pickup, and another arrived so late I'd already left the country.

It depends on where in the world you live, yet it's highly likely that the children you know and love don't wait for long anymore like we used to for the stuff they are coveting. Nor do we.

This affects our mental fitness. Because you have a human brain, you possess a strong negativity bias. It's not your fault; it's the way you are wired. Like millions of others, you've grown used to getting what you want and need almost instantly. Or perhaps you never had to get used to it at all; it's simply native to you, part of being born when and where you were.

Either way, your mental fitness may be negatively affected if you're not conscious of how your brain naturally focuses. In this instance, that could manifest in you, possibly unintentionally, as a tendency to pay more attention to what you *don't* have instead of what you *do* have.

Do you know the song "Never Enough" from the fabulous 2017 movie *The Greatest Showman*? I find myself singing those words all too frequently when demands are being made on me by my teenagers, myself or anyone else who wants more of me than I'm willing or able to give.

We're quickly becoming used to getting what we want when we want it, and these highly altered temporal conditions affect our mental fitness in different ways—fueling a restless sense of impatience and urgency. These are the challenges we face today. However, we must remain mindful of those that await us tomorrow.

Preparing for Abundance

At the time of this writing, the full potential of advanced technologies has not yet reached cruising altitude, but the flight has taxied along the runway, taken off, and the cabin pressurization system has been activated. Futurists are buckled into their seats, eagerly speculating on what awaits us after this significant period of change.

I'm a huge fan of the work of the extraordinary visionaries Ray Kurzweil and Peter Diamandis, and fully and enthusiastically embrace their optimistic, not-so-distant (more like just-around-the-corner) predictions for humanity and the feasibility of ushering in an era of abundance. This is, of course, once we can get over a really shitty, scary stage of leadership predominantly centered on anger, power and greed. When (not if) we do, our health span—the duration of optimal health—will be significantly extended, thus making it a realistic expectation that we will live much longer than we do now.

A long life of abundance... Really? You may be pondering this with unbridled skepticism. Yep, it's close. It's understandable that you can't easily wrap your head around it. When Peter addressed the 13th annual Abundance Summit in March 2025, he declared, "The human species is not used to this level of rapid change." As a result, he advocates for preparing for this "tsunami of change" with the reminder that it was only about a hundred years ago that electricity was applied to a washboard to create the washing machine. Right now, one of the biggest favors you can do for yourself is to shift (if you need to) your frame of reference for the future and be optimistic about the world we're living in because it's exceptionally exciting.

As an eternal optimist, I can't help but wonder what experts such as Martin Seligman and Elaine Fox—known for their research in positive psychology—would say about how pessimists are affected by these seismic shifts. I'm far too biased and inexperienced to guess how someone who sees retirement as "exiting" rather than "exciting" might respond to the gift of time. We will all need to learn how to cope with and flourish in an era of abundance.

One of my favorite mottos is "everything in moderation." I don't just adopt this in relation to eating ice cream on a sunny day, or taking shots of chocolate tequila with fabulous friends gathered around the firepit on a Saturday night, belting out '80s and '90s bangers. I adopt this across the board. Extremes, in my experience, are problematic.

If you eat, cry, work, stress, say, think, feel or care too much, it's bad for you. Yet if you eat, cry, work, stress, say, think, feel or care too little, it's also bad for you. How, then, can we nourish our mental fitness in the upcoming era of abundance? By prioritizing our efforts to develop and maintain it, that's how. We need to become aware of what's out of balance, check on it frequently, and hone the skills to monitor and continually recalibrate throughout our lives.

Mental fitness serves to better us, and then preserve us.

Part Two:
Understanding Mental Fitness

Chapter 4
Togetherness: Bounce With

In the book *Belonging*, acclaimed performance coach Owen Eastwood suggests, "Our ancestors deeply understood our primal need to belong, before psychology or neuroscience gathered the proof. It was visceral to them, part of every day and every decision."

These days, togetherness might be described as a feeling or state of closeness, belonging, unity and connection that goes far beyond merely surviving or safety in numbers. In a transient world where conflict is often sensationalized through online coverage, it's encouraging to understand that differences can be eclipsed by a shared future. The underlying motive for togetherness may have evolved, yet its significance in our lives remains unwavering and constant.

I don't agree that absence makes the heart grow fonder, but I do believe a genuine connection will override distance or time spent apart. Yet that doesn't sound as catchy, does it?! During a visit back home to New Zealand many years ago, I was bemused to see a photo of me stuck on my sister's refrigerator door. She explained she wanted my niece and nephews to grow up with me in their lives on a daily basis, despite my living on the other side of the planet. In that moment, I was flooded with a heartfelt sense of belonging that nourished my soul. Although this loving act wasn't done specifically for me, it benefited me nonetheless, and I wonder to what extent it contributed to the immense, unconditional love I feel for these three extraordinary people. I'm enormously grateful to have them in my life, no matter where any of us are in the world.

Alone vs. Lonely

If you've ever had the misfortune of experiencing a close relationship devoid of genuine depth, you can attest to how painfully lonely that can be. The agonizing despair stemming from a fundamental mismatch is wretched. It will crush one's soul and drain one's spirit. Loneliness isn't about physical proximity; it's about the absence of true connection. Toxic, unfulfilling or shallow bonds create a deep sense of isolation and ultimately underpin the lion's share of human suffering.

For the past several years, I have spent every second Christmas on my own while my kids enjoy the festivities with their dad. The first time, in 2016, was absolutely soul-destroying. I had already drunk myself into a self-wallowing stupor in true Bridget Jones-lonely-birthday-style when I learned George Michael, an English singer-songwriter and record producer, had died, rendering me inconsolable and feeling completely distanced from the many sources of love I had in my life. Thankfully, it was the only Christmas that almost killed me, and the others have actually been quite nourishing. I've embraced solitude by learning to change my perception and choosing to view it as a positive, which has led to the realization that I haven't felt lonely for a long time. (Although I still really miss George!)

Connection

Relationships, whether they're personal or professional, vary in depth and are built on shared experiences, interests or emotional attachment. When positive in nature, they foster trust, empathy and understanding, contributing significantly to your mental fitness as you "bounce with" those in your life. Conversely, when they're absent or turn negative, your mental fitness suffers.

Like all aspects of our lives, connections change over time, shaped by circumstances and personal growth. By actively seeking them out, we can harness the magical quality of a mere moment of connectedness, as Barbara Fredrickson explores in her masterpiece *Love 2.0*. And in the insightful book *Real Love*, Sharon Salzberg, the esteemed cofounder of the Insight Meditation Society, beautifully articulates the tremendous benefits of human connection. She says:

> From our first breath to our last, we're presented again and again with the opportunity to experience deep, lasting and transformative connection with other beings: to love them and be loved by them; to show them our true natures and to recognize theirs. In concert with them, we open our hearts to give and receive. We share joy and compassion, struggles and sorrows, gains and losses. And we learn in our bones what it means to be a part of something bigger than ourselves.

I consider myself to have had an extremely fortunate existence because my suffering is deeply rooted in love as opposed to fear. I haven't grown up without food or clean water, lived in a war zone, or faced brutality or persecution. My life has been a charmed one, of that I'm certain. All the anguish and deep sorrow that has stopped me in my tracks, held me back, rendered me useless, and caused a heartbreaking crisis in my mind—which genuinely felt, in the moment, like the worst pain imaginable—has been because a bond was lost, broken or simply wasn't there when I'd desperately hoped it would be. In any circumstance, the impact created a colossal canyon in my heart, soul and spirit.

On the morning of my sixteenth birthday, I received a letter from my boyfriend. (Yes, I'm old enough that we actually wrote and posted mail back then.) It was a Dear John letter—a bone-crushing birthday moment. Decades later, another gut-wrenching heartbreak struck: As I boarded a plane to return home to the UK, leaving my children on holiday with their dad in Florida, the idea of being thousands of miles away from my precious babies left me feeling utterly destroyed. These are just two of the multiple heart-ripped-from-chest moments I have lived through, yet how lucky I feel to have experienced such enormous love throughout my lifetime; it's truly astounding (and, at times, fucking painful).

Belonging

Belonging relates to acceptance, inclusion and identity within a group or community. Feeling a sense of it means perceiving oneself as a valued member of a collective, which provides emotional security, shapes personal identity, and influences beliefs and behaviors. It is often rooted in shared values, norms and social identities, like culture, religion or interests.

While connection focuses on individual relationships, belonging emphasizes identity and membership within a larger group. It is the equivalent of arriving somewhere and being greeted at the door by an affectionate puppy, whose excited antics signal its absolute delight at seeing you. Connection, on the other hand, is the in-joke, the side-glance packed with meaning, and the intimacy of reciprocated love or like between you and another really cool human.

In *The Joy of Solitude*, psychology professor Robert Coplan coins the term "aloneliness"—a healthy desire for "me time" that sits light years away from the ache of loneliness. That raw hollow has little to do with the physical absence of people; rather, it indicates the soul's craving to bounce with others in a spirit of togetherness embodied by true belonging and connection.

Togetherness

From the primal needs of our ancestors to modern relationships, the importance of togetherness, and its direct association with mental fitness is obvious. Whether we look at tribal cooperation or the contemporary distinctions between connection and belonging, a common thread remains: Humans thrive on shared experiences, comfort and support.

As noted by Stephen Covey in *The 7 Habits of Highly Effective People*, "life is, by nature, highly interdependent." He also likens maximum effectiveness through independence (working alone) as being as effective as playing tennis with a golf club. By acknowledging the innate human need for connection and belonging, we can better empower and enable ourselves to create more contented, fulfilling lives.

> **He aha te mea nui o te ao? He tāngata. He tāngata. He tāngata.**
>
> What is the most important thing in the world? It is people. It is people. It is people.
>
> **—Māori proverb**

Chapter 5
Meaning: Bounce For

Meaning is the lens through which you understand and interpret your life's purpose and significance. Researchers Eric Garland, Norman Farb, Philippe Goldin, and Barbara Fredrickson expand on this definition in their phenomenal paper "Mindfulness Broadens Awareness and Builds Eudaimonic Meaning," which suggests meaning "arises when one's life activities are congruent with deeply held values even under conditions of adversity." In other words, it is profoundly personal, shaped by individual beliefs, experiences and emotions. And your perception of meaning is entirely malleable, shifting over time, perhaps even quite dramatically, as it's influenced by life's ever-changing circumstances. This nuanced understanding is crucial in relation to mental fitness.

What makes your life meaningful? Is it interpretation, purpose or significance? There's no single right answer. It depends on your inclination or preference.

- **Interpretation** involves deeply reflecting on your experiences, beliefs and values to determine what gives your life purpose, fulfillment and direction.

- **Purpose** involves having a sense of direction, motivation and accomplishment that comes from pursuing goals, values or passions through your decisions and actions.
- **Significance** relates to the context, scale and extent to which you affect or influence situations, events and people.

Determining what makes life meaningful often includes asking big questions about the nature of existence and your role in the world. In *Meanings of Life*, Roy Baumeister identifies four critical elements: purpose, efficacy, self-worth and value. He claims if you have these, you are more likely to feel your life has sufficient meaning. In other words, you have something to bounce for, if bouncing represents the act of living. An absence of meaning and purpose "cannot be remedied merely by shuffling the external components of one's life," as Caroline Myss asserts in her New York Times bestseller *Anatomy of the Spirit*.

In essence, a life devoid of meaning may feel rudderless and empty, whereas one infused with purposeful engagement creates a sense of contentment and fulfillment. If life feels unimportant, unclear and pointless, where on earth can the motivation to bounce out of bed in the morning stem from? What can then inspire, delight and intrigue you? If it offers a potential reason for your existence, then it clearly plays an enormously critical role in your mental fitness.

Constructing or Detecting Meaning?

With these diverse facets in mind, an interesting question arises: How do we determine whether our lives have meaning—is it constructed or detected? Do you build it by piecing it together or unlock it, like uncovering a hidden truth?

Do you generate it or facilitate your personal discovery of it? Does it matter how you get there, as long as you do?

The word "constructed" is from the Latin *con*, defined as "with," and *struere*, "to pile up, build." Are we then, when we construct meaning, piling up experiences, beliefs and values like metaphorical bricks, to build our own personal temple? Or let's consider "detect," akin to a detective, someone who uncovers hidden truths. Do we search for clues and patterns to reveal something that preexists, a story already written?

In short, is meaning something we *build with* our lives, or something we *detect within* them? And further, does the work of building, of constructing, give us a sense of agency, of control? Or does detecting point us toward a humbling acknowledgment of a larger, predetermined order?

This linguistic exploration might offer insight. Or perhaps both are true, and the journey incorporates the dance between them. The human experience is, after all, a complex array of building and discovering. Whether meaning is constructed or detected remains to be seen, and the two most common responses I've received to this question, after having asked countless clients, are "it depends" and "both."

If meaning is a creation, then we are the architects of our own existence, crafting narratives and values to navigate the chaos. If it's a discovery, then we are explorers, mapping the contours of an inherent truth.

In relation to mental fitness, what matters most is that your life feels meaningful. Whether that meaning is constructed, detected or a mix of both will depend on context and circumstance. That's it in a nutshell.

Meaning as a Bridge

As we explored at the beginning of this book, our lives unfold in a constant flow, driven by two core motivations: fear and love. Fear prompts us to avoid what's harmful, while love inspires us to seek connection and growth. Meaning isn't just a static idea; it's what we create and discover while these forces are interacting within the broader system of our lives. This interplay is shaped by our personal stories, the larger systems we're part of, and even the language we use. Leaning too much into fear can limit our connections, but focusing solely on love might mean we miss the resilience gained from facing challenges.

Ultimately, meaning acts as a bridge between fear and love, and highlights how our bonds can transform us. By consciously understanding our purpose within life's interconnectedness, we unlock deeper compassion. In this way, meaning isn't just a thought; it's a vital channel for expressing love, fueling our drive, and defining the most fulfilling parts of being human.

Meaning and Balance

A MEANINGFUL LIFE IS a balanced one. Balance is not merely a philosophical construct; it's a fundamental principle woven into the fabric of existence. Consider the natural world: Ecosystems thrive on the delicate contrast of predator and prey, sunlight and shadow, growth and decay. Similarly, our internal world requires maintaining equilibrium between our constructed narratives and other possible truths, between fear and love, and between self and system.

Too much of one element leads to imbalance and a distortion of meaning. So our perception of it requires a balanced perspective. The tension between fear and love, as discussed earlier, is a prime example. Fear, when unchecked, can lead to paralysis and isolation, diminishing our capacity for connection and growth. Meanwhile, love without the grounding of realistic awareness can lead to naivety and excessive vulnerability.

Meaning resides in the delicate balance of the conscious shaping and discovery of our purpose or significance, along with our interpretation of it. Just as a healthy body achieves homeostasis through both rest and activity, nourishment and exertion, a meaningful life likewise depends on a blend of internal and external experiences.

In *The Power of Now*, Eckhart Tolle divides life's journey into two: an outer journey through a horizontal dimension of space and time linked to where you are going and what you are doing, and an inner journey through a vertical dimension of consciousness in the moment, which is how one is able to deepen one's being. He proposes that:

> Your outer journey may contain a million steps; your inner journey only has one: the step you are taking right now. As you become more deeply aware of this one step, you realize that it already contains within itself all the other steps as well as the destination.

It's in the dynamic relationship between our inner and outer worlds, in their continuous feedback loop, that we construct and detect true meaning.

The two worst chapters in my life had similarities, and yet both were linked to meaning in profoundly different ways. A word of caution, though, in case you find personal accounts of mental health struggles upsetting. You might want to skip the next two paragraphs if that is you.

The first, a heavy bout of postnatal depression that required both psychiatric and psychological support, involved bleakness and despair like I'd never previously encountered. It led to fantasies of jumping out of the bathroom window of our rented condominium, eleven floors above the lush Singaporean jungle cover that would obscure the resulting view, to help minimize any suffering I might cause to others. Or it involved me simply wanting to get staggeringly drunk and disappearing into the ocean, between Singapore's busy shipping lanes. These were only fantasies. I never in a million years would have acted upon them, because becoming a mother, despite the brutality of what I was experiencing, gave my life the deepest meaning I'd ever known.

The second, a bout of depression occurring post-COVID-19, was accompanied by a sense of unfathomable meaninglessness, not about my life specifically, but about *all* human life. Another fantasy emerged in which I simply wished eight billion of us did not exist. This full-blown existential crisis became indescribably agonizing. I was so immersed in the downward spiral that I couldn't clearly see it unfold until one day, as a flight my children and I were on made its descent toward our destination, I closed my eyes tightly and wished the plane would crash. It took months of therapy to claw my way out of the mouth of that horrific beast and, as luck would have it, into the open arms of a life brimming with meaning. It was from this darkness that I gained a spirited determination to help people feel better about themselves through my efforts to mainstream mental fitness.

Ultimately, a meaningful life is a balanced one. It is a life where we embrace the interconnectedness of all things, navigating the tension between opposing forces and complementary opposites with curiosity and wisdom. It is a life where we recognize that meaning is not a fixed destination but a dynamic process, a continuous quest for equanimity playing out day by day, moment by moment.

A balanced life is also one of freedom: freedom from fear, freedom of choice, freedom to love. That is precisely what we bounce for!

Chapter 6
Resourcefulness: Bounce Through

According to Merriam-Webster, when someone is resourceful, they are able to meet situations, meaning they are capable of devising ways and means to deal well with new or difficult situations. The TV personality MacGyver might come immediately to mind, with his knack for building a two-way radio out of practically anything. Resourcefulness encompasses your awareness and ability to manage your thoughts, feelings, behavior and energy. It is the metaphorical toolkit you carry around with you to think clearly, feel empowered, and take effective action while on your life journey.

Resourcefulness shows up in the little things that simplify life, like keeping your keys in a specific spot near the door, and in the big things, like maintaining a professional network you can leverage when pivoting to a new role. It is the mental agility that allows you to bounce through any situation you encounter.

Your brain naturally defaults to the well-worn paths of experience, and resourcefulness is the art of creating new ones in anticipation of what might eventually happen. By consciously expanding your repertoire of skills, you broaden your options. Therefore, when the time comes to react and respond, you do so with an increased capacity to bounce through, nurturing your mental fitness regardless of what happens.

To illustrate, let's play a little game... Think of the word "conductor." Whatever picture or thought sprang into your mind is influenced by your personal history—that is, your life experiences up to now.

You might have imagined the conductor of an orchestra, creating harmony by directing multiple musicians. Or perhaps you thought of an old-fashioned bus conductor, assisting passengers to safety and helping them navigate their journey with ease. Maybe you visualized a lightning conductor, employed to prevent destruction and channel an abundance of energy.

Your instantaneous response is possible due to your brain's sophisticated executive function, which determines the most effective and efficient path to lead you down with super-quick processing. Now your keys are consistently near the door (and you know where the spare set lives), and you're frequently interacting with your network in a way that feels genuine rather than contrived and inauthentic.

In essence, it's possible to conduct the orchestra of your thoughts, feelings and behavior; navigate your journey with ease; and channel the abundance of energy you have as a dynamic, living creature. You can have it all. Ta-da! (Mic drop moment.) What a clever person you are!

When life is flowing smoothly and going according to plan, you are probably leveraging many practices, all of which are serving you well. They might be simple daily rituals, like a consistent wake-up time or washing routine, or more complex ones. Perhaps you notice how your energy spikes after engaging activities increase your dopamine levels, and you therefore harness that to be productive. Or you know an encounter with a certain person will more often than not derail your attention with feelings of irritation, unfairness, disdain or full-blown fury. So you plan accordingly, perhaps deciding to take the dog for a walk or phone a friend immediately after the encounter. By employing resourcefulness, you can accurately anticipate what's coming and plan for the best way to mitigate the damage.

Managing Mental Fitness

As a teenager, I belonged to a surf lifesaving club on the east coast of New Zealand, in the aptly named Bay of Plenty. I took part in only two rescue operations, but they left lasting impressions on me. In one instance, I saved a dog caught in a riptide. The other took place on a day when the beach was officially closed due to a fierce storm and involved dozens of us, including a search and rescue helicopter team. Unfortunately, it ended in defeat and tragedy. The body washed up farther along the coast about three weeks later. His name was Patrick, and none of us will ever forget that most horrific ordeal.

Ever since that day, I've had a thing (or as my kids would say, I get the "ick") about the phrasing "you saved my life" or "you're a real lifesaver," which I humbly admit is a compliment sometimes given to me in my role as a professional coach. My usual response is gently pointing out that unless I am performing CPR, I'm not saving a life—I'm simply facilitating insight and creating empowering conditions conducive to change. Yes, I've clocked thousands of coaching hours and honed my craft in ways that make it valuable to my clients as they experience growth and transformation, and I adore what I do because it's exceptionally rewarding to be a part of their journey. However, I do not exaggerate my contribution. Each and every individual is fully responsible for their own life, which I do not save.

As an insatiable consumer of self-development materials, I also have a second thing that gives me the ick: when a person implies their content is a real game-changer, a lifesaver, that it's the only thing you'll ever need to do (buy!) to be set free to live among the unicorns in a glittery, shiny land of rainbows and laughter. Fuck right off! Because I want to avoid being perceived as someone who is in it mainly for their own financial gain or as if I have tapped into some mystical formula catapulting me far from the harshness of human suffering, my intent is to remain transparent with you about my own mental fitness management. It requires dedicated, consistent application of the Better Mental Fitness Framework. It's a practice, not a potion.

Here's an example. Despite the vast majority of my attention revolving around mental fitness, most mornings I need to process what my subconscious has surfaced during the night in vivid dreams centered on deep insecurities. I realized a while ago that I needed time, a buffer, so I could process this uncontrollable mental activity and gently let it go before getting on with the day. I call it the "morning margin."

In 2004, Drew Barrymore and Adam Sandler starred in *50 First Dates*, a gorgeously sweet movie. Every time Lucy (Barrymore) goes to sleep, her short-term memory resets, and so Henry (Sandler) endeavors to win her heart anew each day. As part of my morning margin routine, I channel my inner Henry to cater to my inner Lucy, because most days I wake up and it's as if I've forgotten everything unless I make a conscious effort to focus on mental fitness.

That is how strong my natural urge to default to autopilot is, which seems far more "human doing" than "human being." This has remained true despite my commitment to self-development, which began with therapy in the '90s after my first marriage broke up. The learning is ongoing, has no end in sight, and is nonlinear. The lyrics of "Persuasion," by Tim Finn, Kiwi singer and former member of global sensation Crowded House, ring true, where he talks about how a constant battle runs through his head. These days, mental fitness is my anchor, boat and navigational chart. It is not and will never become the ocean I set sail on, which remains enigmatic and unpredictable.

In a VUCA world—a term meaning volatile, uncertain, complex and ambiguous that is commonly attributed to the iconic Warren Bennis—each of us embodies our own version of VUCA, which I think of as vulnerable, unsettled, complicated and anxious.

One of my lovely clients, Hazel, says if you ask someone how they are and their response is "fine," it actually stands for fucked-up, insecure, neurotic and emotional!

It's hard to be human, and as I sail around on my inner ocean, I'm glad of the support mental fitness offers. Yet I hold no false assumptions it will miraculously eradicate stormy seas. Even MacGyver couldn't do that!

Practical Resourcefulness

Being resourceful takes effort. By deliberately harnessing cognitive and emotional skills to develop awareness, we can "reconnect with our essential nature and nurture that spark into a brilliant flame." This is how Tsoknyi Rinpoche describes key elements of the practice of transcendent wisdom in *Open Heart, Open Mind*.

Resourcefulness is also broad and far-reaching, mirroring the dynamic and complex nature of your lived experience. It can be understood through three fundamental components:

- **Behavior:** what you do
- **Emotions:** how you feel
- **Thoughts:** what you think

These form a handy "BET" mnemonic, which I refer to with a cheesy, but memorable, "You BET!" Whenever you see references in this book to thinking, feeling and behavior, picture yourself shouting You BET! Welcome to the cheese factory.

The fact you've picked up *Better* demonstrates you have an aptitude for resourcefulness, in that you are open, curious and growth-oriented. Resourcefulness is the deliberate, practical application of mental fitness, requiring continuous effort, awareness and commitment. It is both proactive and reactive, meaning it's not just about preparing for what may or may not happen next but is also inextricably tied to being mentally present in the moment.

Mindfulness vs. Mindlessness

All of this brings us to the topic of mindfulness, which is an excellent resource to draw upon. It's free, it's readily available, and you can become mindful while continuing with whatever you're feeling, doing or thinking, just by adding a subtle layer of noticing.

Here's the kicker: mindfulness isn't necessarily going to be the go-to resource to cultivate mental fitness. In their book *The Buddha Pill*, psychologists Miguel Farias and Catherine Wikholm question whether meditative practices, including mindfulness, change us for the better. I share their view that it simply is not suitable for every situation. I vividly recall times in my life when, for a variety of reasons, practicing mindfulness was way too painful, and I consciously opted to zone out and embrace numbness to get me through the day.

There was the time I had a big, grown-up, corporate job and was attempting to hide the early stages of my sixth pregnancy, because in no way did I wish to announce my state to the world, even while enduring horrendous morning sickness. For a few weeks, all I could face eating was a McDonald's Filet-O-Fish, and it wouldn't have been an enormous surprise to have given birth to a baby resembling Ronald McDonald. And there was another time when I was going through a heart-wrenching break-up with one of the greatest loves of my life, and I consciously chose to exist mindlessly for a while since being connected to the present was far too painful. Melting into a bottle of wine and binge-watching a show was the much easier and preferred alternative.

All of this being said, mindfulness is good for fostering resourcefulness and resilience, most of the time.

You *are* resourceful, and you are capable of broadening that trait even further. However, it will take vigilance and effort on your part. And while developing your resourcefulness might not save your life, it will unquestionably make you better prepared for whatever happens.

Chapter 7
Resilience: Bounce Back

According to renowned neuropsychologist Rick Hanson, resilience is our ability to cope with adversity and push through challenges in the pursuit of opportunities, and it goes hand in hand with wellbeing because they promote each other in an upward spiral.

At the time I began my research on resilience, I also happened to be navigating the final chapter of an important relationship, and it was a period jam-packed with emotion. I was shocked, mortified, bereft, devastated, livid and just plain sad, all while raising two young children thousands of miles away from my family. But even before that, I had exhibited enormous resilience without realizing it.

Not long after we celebrated the new millennium, my biological clock began ticking as loud as Big Ben. After an initial miscarriage, I became pregnant again relatively quickly. My excitement was smashed to bits when, one evening, during my picturesque commute home by boat along the River Thames in London, I experienced severe abdominal pain. After being rushed to the hospital, I learned the first of my two ectopic pregnancies was well underway.

The next part is hard to write, not just because of the emotional trauma, but because it was so intense that my brain blocked it out altogether. I later came to understand the fragility of the hippocampus and the brain's exceptionally clever ability to shut it down in order to protect it—which is what happened to me. According to my lovely sister, I was completely hysterical when I called her from the other side of the world, after having been told I was about to undergo surgery in which they would remove both of my fallopian tubes. She pleaded with me to get a second opinion. I took her advice, and the result was the preservation of one of the tubes—a single, precious lifeline that precariously held my future hopes and dreams of motherhood. This experience taught me that we humans have a remarkable capacity to bounce back in the face of adversity, setbacks and challenges, whether they be physical, mental or emotional, and we can frequently surprise ourselves.

This story is predominantly about resilience since I overcame this horror and went on to try again (having nine pregnancies in all). It also touches on meaning, given my inextinguishable yearning for motherhood, and on togetherness; had it not been for this special sisterly bond—forged in unconditional love—I might have lost the opportunity to become a mother on that horrific day, at least in the biological sense. It still surprises me I cannot recall that conversation, which remains one of the most significant of my life.

In the previous chapter, I touched on the proactive nature of resourcefulness and the benefit of building skills and capabilities to help you through your daily life.

Resilience is primarily reactive. Something has to have happened to knock you out, down or over for you to demonstrate it. It is situational and highly contextual. Yet, it is also a skill that can be built in advance, in readiness for what might happen. I would suggest there's no such thing as a "resilient person," just like there is no such thing as an "angry person," only a person feeling anger. This is better framed as a "person being resilient" or a "person demonstrating resilience."

If resilience is the ability to bounce back, what capabilities make that possible? How can we accept reality, derive meaning from hardship, and improvise solutions out of what might sometimes seem like thin air?

Let's explore a simple yet effective resilience framework you can practice. It has three dimensions of equal importance: balance, mindfulness and emotion regulation.

Balance

Humans function as intricate systems within systems, constantly responding to and interacting with the world around us. To manage this complexity, our bodies rely on homeostasis—a critical biological mechanism that enables living organisms to adapt and maintain a stable internal balance despite constant changes in their external environment. It works by regulating various physiological processes, such as body temperature, blood pressure, glucose levels, and pH balance, to ensure optimal conditions for the organism's survival and proper functioning.

In the human body, homeostasis is achieved through the coordination of multiple organ systems and feedback mechanisms. The goal is to achieve a dynamic equilibrium by constantly adjusting internal conditions to keep them within a narrow and optimal range. This process is essential for maintaining good health since deviations from the normal range can lead to illness or disease.

But our necessity for balance goes far beyond our physical state, as illustrated by clinical psychologist Christopher K. Germer in *The Mindful Path to Self-Compassion.* He says, "Most spiritually minded people see the need for *both* approaches in their lives: to be uplifted by a transcendent ideal and yet to remain grounded in ordinary reality."

Nothing overrides the demand all living beings have for this equilibrium. When anything is out of balance, it causes problems, be they big, like climate change, or small, like tripping as you walk.

Resilience is about bouncing back, but balance is the fixed anchor point to which we return.

Mindfulness

Jon Kabat-Zinn defines mindfulness as "awareness that arises through paying attention, on purpose, in the present moment, and non-judgmentally." That's it; super simple. What happens next is where things get a bit more interesting. As compulsive sense-making, meaning-making humans, we scrutinize, judge, critique and apply a whole heap of other stuff onto what mindfulness offers, whether it's being perceived as a state or a trait.

Why is that? Well, let's be honest. It's remarkably hard for us to stick to being human; we prefer to be human beings *and* human doings. We're always doing something, and a lot of it is happening unconsciously without us even noticing.

I predict it will be fundamentally important, as we move into the next part of history and our lived experience becomes intricately intertwined with technology, to acquire the ability to practice mindfulness readily. This change will galvanize an entirely new era for human-machine interaction and potentially give us a lot more free time. Therefore, the ability to shift from human doings to human beings will have a direct effect on our overall mental fitness. A swift, disruptive departure from the aftermath of the Industrial Revolution might push us well beyond our ability to be resilient if we don't learn to value (or tolerate) being over doing.

We might discover it's useful to emulate our pets, finding within ourselves the ability to derive contentment and fulfillment from just existing. One of the extraordinary mindfulness teachers I've studied with, Fay Adams, frequently uses a powerfully beautiful phrase in guided meditation, saying, "Nowhere to go, nothing to do." It would do us all good to repeat this mantra daily and then breathe.

Mindfulness has been practiced for centuries as a key aspect of Buddhism, and contemplative science has continued to extend the concept beyond any specific culture or belief system, with a focus on its positive gains for many (though not all). The living legend Jon Kabat-Zinn has been at the forefront of Western mindfulness for years. I've heard countless stories from people who are indebted to him for his work, and I gladly claim my place in that vast community for all he has achieved through mainstreaming mindfulness. In *Full Catastrophe Living*, he explains the natural progression of the journey toward greater health and wellbeing, and how "Awareness, insight and indeed health as well, ripen on their own if we are willing to pay attention in the moment and remember that we only have moments to live."

Emotion Regulation

Let's get one thing straight first and foremost: it's emotion regulation, not emotional regulation. (Confusing these terms is one of my pet peeves.)

You cannot *control* your emotions, and any attempts to do so are an utter waste of your time and energy that will probably make things worse in the long run. However, *regulating* emotion, both proactively and in response to any situation that contains an emotional trigger, is a skill worth its weight in gold. This means you behave in a grounded, measured manner rather than inadvertently reverting to your three-year-old self in full-blown tantrum mode. Neuropsychiatrist Daniel Siegel uses his "Hand Model of the Brain" to demonstrate a valuable technique to understand what is going on in the brain when we are triggered.

To develop your skills, start by becoming aware of which emotions cause you the most discomfort. Beyond the obvious choices, this means acknowledging those you might be experiencing unbeknownst to yourself. Once you've identified them, you can increase your capacity to regulate them more quickly when they arise. This is proactive emotion regulation, a hallmark of mental flexibility—even if the idea sounds paradoxical at first.

If you're looking to build your capacity even further, Daniel Goleman and Richard Davidson share good news in *The Science of Mediation*, reporting that long-term meditation strengthens functional connectivity in the brain in a circuit that is important for emotion regulation, lessening stress reactivity and cortisol levels.

You might need professional help with this, and I wholeheartedly agree with Owen O'Kane, author of the bestselling book *How to Be Your Own Therapist*, who believes every single one of us could benefit from therapy. In fact, I regularly encounter individuals whose stories remain largely unresolved. I believe—with enormous hope and everything crossed—that one of the positive outcomes of this era will be that more people will use therapeutic services. In my opinion, this area would benefit from continuing to rely on human patient-client interaction, rather than AI, to be most effective.

However, even if you cannot see a therapist, you can still develop your skills. As you increase your awareness, you will notice more opportunities to regulate your emotions. There are many techniques you can try. Some of the boosters in this book are based on the work of Stanford professor James J. Gross, who is often thought of as the father of emotion regulation. He emphasizes "the events that grip us emotionally are not always the ones that we should focus our energies on," which is a refreshing reminder of just how easily we can get sucked into the emotional aspects of our lives.

My journey to improve my emotion regulation involved significant learning and personal insight. It took me years to learn how to turn down the volume on the boombox of my emotions, and a mute button is not a feature on my make and model, though I do have controls for treble and bass and can adjust the sound quite well now.

Toward the end of 2018, I submitted the dissertation for my master of science degree in Studies in Mindfulness to the University of Aberdeen. If you have ever completed an intense, time-consuming course of study, you will probably vigorously nod in agreement when I describe a few euphoric weeks of uttering "Never again!" that was swiftly followed by a period of learning bliss, during which I could discover and absorb new concepts at my leisure, entirely untethered.

At that time, I was salivating over the information I obtained from attending the Eighth Annual World Business and Executive Coaching Summit. While there, I participated in a powerful workshop given by an extraordinary scholar and Stanford University professor named Shirzad Chamine, during which I gained deep insight into my inner emotional world. As a result of that experience, I read his book *Positive Intelligence*, completed the free online assessment, and took part in a training program he created specifically for coaches. Through it, I improved my ability to identify toxicity in relationships and take ownership of the role I was playing.

There are certain aspects I don't particularly like about myself, including that I am a highly sensitive person—someone with what psychologist Elaine Aron refers to as sensory-processing sensitivity—which, quite frankly, is bloody annoying. Because of it, I need to manage what I can only describe as excessive fragility, and it means protecting my poor little heart from what potentially destroys me, just as Superman avoids kryptonite. It's sad; I've lost relationships because of it. The upside is that I cherish my valued inner circle, which is filled with people who nurture my mental fitness lovingly, tirelessly and almost effortlessly.

Managing high sensitivity is, like most things, an ongoing effort, since becoming aware of it is not the same as doing something about it. To meet this challenge, I constantly adopt the pragmatic approach championed by Angela Duckworth, author of *Grit*, thinking: Well, this didn't work, that didn't work, that didn't work, that didn't work... But I haven't tried this yet!

It may be coincidental, but my life has been profoundly shaped by the teachings of two Stanford University professors mentioned in this chapter: Shirzad Chamine and James Gross. I'm not sure whether their work intersects. Still, in my mind, they're the best of friends, spending sunny Californian weekends together with their families, friends and dogs, engaged in lively conversations about the emotional terrain of being human. Or maybe they are neighbors in the gorgeous town of Carlsbad (the home of TaylorMade for any golf enthusiasts) and are surf buddies as often as their busy schedules allow, embodying the spirit of nowhere to go and nothing to do.

Odd daydreams aside, as one of the leading experts on the topic of resilience, Rick Hanson describes this cornerstone as having the ability to thrive on good days and survive the bad ones. As such, resilience is the umbrella, and while an umbrella may conveniently prevent you from getting wet, it can't stop the rain, nor was it designed to.

Chapter 8
Wellbeing: Bounce Well

In the twenty-first century, particularly in the wake of the COVID-19 pandemic, I have seen a renewed emphasis on reclaiming our wellbeing. We're actively building a broader, deeper understanding of what it means to be healthy by blending the art and science of being human—something we've done exceptionally well for centuries—through this relatively new lens.

A curious and open spirit embraces reality, recognizing perfectionism—including our outdated notions of "normal"—is an unrealistic pursuit. In fact, being a bit of a wonky donkey is effectively as normal as you can get when it comes to being human. We all possess abnormalities, and we are all meant to learn and grow, which is precisely what adventurers do best.

Defining Wellbeing

THANKFULLY, WELLBEING as a concept has gained the attention of mainstream audiences, whether you spell it as wellbeing, well-being or well being. (It's all the same thing.) When concepts evolve, a rush of new opinions, definitions and experts follow in hot pursuit. Wellbeing is no different and, as a result, there are numerous versions and variations available to digest.

Here are some useful definitions to consider:

- Subjective wellbeing is defined by the Organisation for Economic Co-operation and Development on their website as "Good mental states, including all of the various evaluations, positive and negative, that people make of their lives and the affective reactions of people to their experiences."
- Psychologist Carol Ryff has described psychological wellbeing, through what are commonly known as the Ryff Scales, as six dimensions of challenged thriving: self-acceptance, positive relations with others, environmental mastery, autonomy, purpose in life, and personal growth.
- Psychologists Richard Ryan and Edward Deci describe wellbeing as "a complex construct that concerns optimal experience and functioning. Current research on well-being has been derived from two general perspectives: the hedonic approach, which focuses on happiness and defines well-being in terms of pleasure attainment and pain avoidance; and the eudaimonic approach, which focuses on meaning and self-realization and defines well-being in terms of the degree to which a person is fully functioning" in their 2001 review of research on hedonic and eudaimonic wellbeing.
- Sapien Labs, founded by Tara Thiagarajan, describes mental wellbeing on its website as "the ability to handle life and its various stresses and challenges." They offer an excellent free online assessment, the Mental Health Quotient, or MHQ, which provides a snapshot of your self-perception along with six dimensions of mental function that reflect your mental wellbeing. They emphasize the MHQ is not a measure

of happiness or life satisfaction. You could, for example, be experiencing very difficult or sad circumstances, but nonetheless have the skills to cope, and therefore have a high level of wellbeing. At the time of this writing, the dimensions rated in the MHQ are adaptability and resilience, cognition, drive and motivation, mind-body connection, mood and outlook, and social self.

- The iconic and adored father of positive psychology, Martin Seligman, established the PERMA model, in which he describes wellbeing as having five measurable elements: positive emotion, engagement, relationships, meaning and accomplishment.

For the Better Mental Fitness Framework, we adopt a simplified definition of wellbeing, describing it as "bouncing well, with inner harmony, vitality and life satisfaction." This is sufficiently broad to cover the various academic models while remaining open to your own interpretation.

Beyond Happiness

To be happy or not to be happy? A better question is how you might attain contentment and fulfillment in your life because of, and sometimes even despite, the circumstances. That is what mental fitness seeks to answer.

While the sentiment of happiness is truly wonderful, the word itself is too crammed with complexity to convey the source, essence and applications of mental fitness clearly. Although I have enormous admiration for initiatives like Action for Happiness, the Happiness Lab, the Happier Lives Institute, the World Happiness Report, and the World Happiness Summit, along with books like Gretchen Rubin's *The Happiness Project*, I largely avoid using the term, as I mentioned earlier. When it comes to mental fitness, it's reasonable to assume happiness serves as an entirely appropriate synonym for wellbeing. This is illustrated in Richard Layard's book, *Happiness*, where he observes the modern challenge is "to master ourselves and to give us more of the happiness that we all want." However, in this case, "wellbeing" could easily be substituted for "happiness" and still make complete sense, which is what I would recommend.

It's essential to consider wellbeing as a distinct component of mental fitness, not merely an umbrella term or an aggregation of the other four cornerstones (togetherness, meaning, resourcefulness and resilience). This is because the dynamic, unpredictable nature of our stream of consciousness subtly shifts from moment to moment. Consequently, one might report a strong sense of togetherness, meaning, resourcefulness and resilience, yet still experience unhappiness if their sense of wellbeing is impaired for whatever reason. This is similar to how your level of mental wellbeing might score highly in the MHQ even when you're experiencing adversity.

As with most components of internal lived experience, measuring wellbeing belongs in the same camp as the proverbial "How long is a piece of string?" In the bounce score assessment (which was covered in "The Concept of Bounce" on page 7), the question related to this cornerstone is: "How would you rate your sense of inner harmony, vitality and life satisfaction?" This really cannot do it justice, but nor could a twenty-nine-thousand-question survey! Your response to either may vary greatly from one moment to the next, just as your life does.

That being said, it's still worthwhile to ask yourself that question, and it's also entirely reasonable to respond to it based purely on a momentary intuition you could refer to as a "guess-essment" (totally made-up word). It might be as quick as politely responding, "Very well, thank you," when asked how you are doing (yet resoundingly more honest). Just as beauty is in the eye of the beholder, wellbeing is a self-determined state.

The A–E of Wellbeing

If you want to assess your current mental state, I recommend addressing five factors, listed from A to E, that are commonly associated with wellbeing:

- **Autonomy:** The capacity to govern your actions, attention and choices.
- **Balance:** A sense of equilibrium between different aspects of living, and equanimity toward life events.
- **Compassion:** The desire and means to alleviate suffering for yourself and others.
- **Dynamism:** The acceptance that your existence is unpredictable, complex and in a constant state of change.
- **Energy:** The ability to manage your energy effectively—from how you harness it to its quality and quantity as you transmit it into the world.

I mentioned in the previous chapter how annoying it is to be a highly sensitive person (and not just to me, since it affects the people around me). There's a touch too much going on in my inner world at any point, and it manifests in multiple ways. I attribute the voices in my head, tinnitus, adrenal fatigue, anosmia and three failed marriages to it, to name but a few! It also has its upsides, such as my intuitive method of coaching and my ability to feel joy vicariously, among other benefits.

I use the A–E of Wellbeing as a quick checklist (a moodometer, so to speak) to help me better understand *what* is happening *while* it is happening, with no set agenda other than to notice. In this sense, the list provides a scaffold for dynamic mindfulness because I'm "being here, not there, and seeing what's here." Doing this may either generate new insight, initiate change as I alter my behavior, or simply lead to acceptance of what is. For example, I was asked to reschedule an appointment to start fifteen minutes later than we had agreed, and I was given plenty of notice, so of course it was completely okay to do so. I arrived punctually at the rescheduled time and then waited for yet another fifteen minutes before I was seen. Since I'm not a fan of lateness, it put me in an Oscar the Grouch–like state for the next three to four hours, which I'm at peace with, because riding with the mood suits me better than adding any further layers to it. I prefer to let myself do so, since it helps me recalibrate more quickly every time; it's fighting my mood that causes problems, because that can all go downhill swiftly.

The A–E of Wellbeing supports me in staying grounded while I observe which factors are being affected and how that influences my feelings, thoughts and behavior. As a recovering control freak, this ability has made a massive difference to my sense of wellbeing over the years.

Mood and emotion, though often used interchangeably, are distinctly different. Since both affect your sense of inner harmony, it is useful to understand the difference between the temporary surge of an emotion and the longer-running nature of a mood.

Picture this: You're doing something that doesn't require much of your attention—washing dishes, showering, driving the car—and simultaneously listening to your favorite playlist on Spotify, which you've set to shuffle. Your playlist selection and its overall vibe represent your mood. It's a prolonged state that can last for minutes, hours, days or even longer.

Emotions, on the other hand, are intense and can be short-lived; they're the individual songs that spontaneously pop up on shuffle and instantly catapult you into joy, sorrow, rage or ecstasy. You know precisely why you feel the way you do as it starts to play, since each song is packed with context. Essentially, mood is to emotion as Spotify is to songs.

I love prompting Spotify to deliver music to suit my mood or whatever I'm doing. My Spotify use changes often, and at times for no apparent reason—it just *is what it is*. Sometimes I'm not even in the mood for music.

As the soundtrack of life changes, so too does my mood and sense of wellbeing. For me personally, mood affects my wellbeing more than temporary emotions do. That might not be the case for you. Therefore, being able to distinguish between them provides insight into what affects your mental fitness. As a result, you may decide to create your own version of the A–E of Wellbeing; yours might even end up being an A–G, L, P or even X, Y or Z! Whatever makes you bounce well. It's your adventure, after all!

Part Three:
Cultivating Mental Fitness

Chapter 9

Embarking on Your Better Mental Fitness Journey

Now that we have established you are the most important person in your universe (and that it's absolutely, completely okay, or even essential, to think that way), it's time to kick-start the process of nourishing your mental fitness. By the end of this chapter, you will have selected a profile (although this is optional), identified your preferred cadence for completing the boosters, and selected a start date that aligns with what's currently going on in your life.

How? That's most definitely the question! To help you get started, let's talk about each of these elements.

How the Boosters Work

First, let's get into the nuts and bolts of the boosters:

- There are a total of forty-two boosters plus the ten-stage Mental Fitness Rocket Booster.
- Each one is presented the same way, so the format fades into the background as you become familiar with them.

- The structure lends itself to easy reuse. You can quickly find the sections on how to prepare, how long it takes, and what to do, making it simple to revisit a booster without rereading the entire thing.
- Generally, getting results from a booster isn't dependent on completing any of the others, so you can dip in and out randomly if that's your preference. When it is necessary to do another booster first, the prerequisite is clearly stated.
- You may periodically want to recalculate your bounce score to help you determine which boosters are most beneficial to you at the moment. If you don't recall how to do that, refer to "The Concept of Bounce" on page 7.

It's fairly common for people to check their bounce score and instantly spot one or two specific areas needing attention. If that applies to you, the "Cornerstone Guide" on page 191 will help easily pinpoint the boosters you might like to try first, based on what you want to work on.

Boosters are designed to positively contribute toward your mental fitness in the same way exercise and movement impact your physical fitness. One session in the gym does not make you a bodybuilder, nor will attempting a booster once change your life. The goal is to maintain, develop or improve the levels of contentment and fulfillment you experience daily, and in turn, that will affect your overall mental fitness.

Clarify Your Mission

Depending on how your brain works, this book may inadvertently create a temporary paradox: the very effort to feel better can initially make you feel worse. Your mean inner voices may chime in with their cruel perspectives, chastising you for a colorful range of reasons, predominantly associated with what you are or are not doing (guilt) or who you are or are not (shame). To combat this paradox and to (a) make you feel a bit better about the voices, and (b) justify providing yourself with the opportunity, time and space to try out these boosters, I've created four made-up, completely nonscientific profiles designed to help you clarify how to proceed from here.

Each profile suggests a primary motivation style of: approach ("I want to make things better") or avoidance ("I don't want things to deteriorate further"), and a primary motivation goal, which may or may not resonate with you. It also includes a mantra-like mission to serve as a gentle reminder of what it is you're trying to achieve as you work through the boosters.

Profile 1. Guide Me

The Guide Me profile is for you if you see a lengthy list of boosters and the instantaneous sense of overwhelm sets off a mini explosion in your head. You may think, "I don't know what to do. Help me!"

Your primary motivation style:	Approach
Your primary motivation goal:	Purpose
Your mission:	Discern and discard

Follow these steps:

1. Calculate your current bounce score.
2. Use your score to decide in which order to work through the boosters. Is there an area to prioritize first?
3. Try the boosters to discern which ones work best for you and that you will use going forward. Discard the rest.
4. Recalculate your bounce score to determine whether this approach helped you.

Profile 2. Convince Me

The Convince Me profile is for you if you see a lengthy list of boosters and your rebellious inner child screeches, "Nope, not gonna do it, and you can't make me!" because you hate being told what to do (even by yourself). You may think, "I need clarity and context. Inspire me!"

Your primary motivation style:	Avoidance
Your primary motivation goal:	Autonomy
Your mission:	Investigate and ignite

Follow these steps:

1. If you want to, calculate your bounce score.
2. Just give the boosters a try and if you get anything out of it, it's a bonus. No pressure; it's your call.
3. Investigate whether any of this is making (or ignites) a positive difference (or might in future).
4. If you want to, recalculate your bounce score to determine whether this approach helped you.

Profile 3. Comfort Me

The Comfort Me profile is for you if you see a lengthy list of boosters and begin freaking out that you will miss out on something unless you're hypervigilant and paying close attention, unintentionally provoking a stress response. You may think, "I have major FOMO. Reassure me!"

Your primary motivation style:	Avoidance
Your primary motivation goal:	Mastery
Your mission:	Explore and empower

Follow these steps:

1. Calculate your bounce score.
2. Choose your start date.

3. Let the exploration begin and feel empowered as you implement the boosters!
4. Recalculate your bounce score to determine whether this approach helped you.

Profile 4. Support Me

The Support Me profile is for you if you see a lengthy list of boosters and sigh in resignation as you contemplate whether you will ever truly be in control of your relentless, ever-increasing list of things to do. You may think, "I'll add this to my very long to-do list. Enable me!"

Your primary motivation style:	Approach
Your primary motivation goal:	Mastery
Your mission:	Validate and verify

Follow these steps:

1. Calculate your bounce score.
2. Choose your start date, preferably today or tomorrow.
3. Validate and verify by answering these questions: Have I harnessed the right booster and in the right manner?
4. After you try each booster, make notes about it for future reference, including how to adapt it to suit your needs better.
5. Recalculate your bounce score to determine whether this approach helped you.

Choose Your Preferred Cadence

ONCE YOU HAVE DECIDED which profile suits you best and therefore what your mission is (or once you have determined you don't need to align with one), you can select your cadence and off you go.

Choosing the cadence—the speed with which you will work through the boosters—is another aspect with no right or wrong approach. Simply choose what will serve you best in relation to your personal sense of urgency, the amount of time you have available, the priority you are currently giving your mental fitness, and any other factors. You can't make a mistake with this. And if you select a cadence that doesn't work well for whatever reason, you can change it at any time and it's not going to break anything.

There are many potential cadences for implementing the boosters. You might want to go as fast as Usain Bolt or you might want to do a marathon.

My only recommendation concerns the Mental Fitness Rocket Booster found in Chapter 11—allow time for your subconscious mind to absorb the content and percolate for a little while. The easiest way to do that is to sleep on it. Therefore, plan on taking a minimum of ten days to complete all ten stages of the rocket booster.

Once you have decided on a cadence, all that's left is to choose a start date if you haven't already and... Ready, set, go! You're on a mission. I wish you well on your mental fitness journey.

Chapter 10
Better Mental Fitness Boosters

Each of the boosters in the Better Mental Fitness Framework follows the same format, sharing a consistent layout to make them easily digestible as you experiment with them and hopefully discover your future favorites!

What it's good for	The cornerstone supported by the booster.
What it is	A high-level snapshot, so you can swiftly decide if this booster matches your current needs.
What it does	The intended value or impact.
How to prepare	A quick check to ready yourself (inner world) and your environment (outer world).
How long it takes	An approximate duration to calibrate with your schedule.
What to do	The clear, actionable, step-by-step instructions.

How it works — A brief nod to the mechanics of why or how this initiates a shift.

How to explore further — A deeper inquiry for those eager to venture along the proverbial bunny trail.

How it came to be — The backstory for the booster or a personal application to bring it to life.

A quick visual reference for each booster indicates the cornerstone it develops, the approximate amount of time needed, as well as which ones can be done when you need to take immediate action. Here is what each icon means:

 Cultivates Togetherness

 Cultivates Meaning

 Cultivates Resourcefulness

 Cultivates Resilience

 Cultivates Wellbeing

 Less than 10 minutes

 Less than 30 minutes

 More than 30 minutes

 Produces Immediate Results

Booster 1. 10K-Day Plan

What it's good for: Cultivating meaning

What it is: This method for big-picture thinking clarifies your vision.

What it does: It sparks insight, motivation and actions that benefit you long term.

How to prepare: Complete "Booster 17. Formula of Fulfillment" on page 113.

How long it takes: 45–60 minutes

What to do:

1. Using a free online date calculator, figure out the date 10,000 days from now.
2. Pick a significant date close to that by rounding up or down—it could be a milestone birthday, an anniversary, or any other date that resonates—to bring your distant future into relatable focus.
3. Imagine having a conversation with the version of you who exists on the significant date you chose.
4. Revisit your Formula of Fulfillment and coax your "future you" to share some invaluable insights with the "current you":
   - What will future you think matters most?
   - What will future you feel passionate about?
   - What will future you uphold as core values?
5. Decide what you will continue, amend, start or stop to identify actions future you might encourage current you to embrace.

How it works: This method connects you to your vision and purpose by bypassing immediate distractions, allowing you to explore deeper aspirations and lay the groundwork for a future you'll genuinely appreciate.

How to explore further: Go deeper by engaging with future you to set meaningful goals. Use this 10K-day plan as a compass pointing toward your true north, while remembering the objectives might change on your journey.

Craving more wisdom on time? Dive into Oliver Burkeman's *Four Thousand Weeks*, in which he asks, "What would it mean to spend the only time you ever get in a way that truly feels as though you are making it count?"

How it came to be: My curiosity about numbers exploded when I was working at Rabobank in London and Utrecht with a trading system called Kondor+. Using its functionality, it was possible to calculate trade durations quickly, and on quiet days, we'd create various scenarios just for fun. This inspired a novel and relatively quirky 10,000-day celebration of my life (at around 27 years, 4 months) at a Hammersmith pub in early 1999. It was such a brilliant party with an electric atmosphere, great people, and zero birthday gifts. My friend's brother even showed up with bagpipes. It was epic.

A few years later, still hooked on numbers, I developed a professional interest in creatively harnessing different versions of the self across the temporal realms of past, present and future. I would have coaching clients write love letters to their current selves from their future selves. This was back in the digital Stone Age: I'd provide an envelope, we'd seal it, and I'd eventually mail it months later, with an actual stamp! The fabulous news is that future you is likely to be remarkably kind and understanding. They've been there, done that, and they're in your corner. So, if you're feeling a bit hesitant about building your 10K-Day Plan, remember you're partnering with someone who has your back and is continuously cheering you on.

More recently, I crafted a 10K-Day Plan that hits my eightieth birthday. It's the perfect time to decide whether I'm finally ready for retirement or if the adventure to mainstream mental fitness just keeps calling. An unexpected, very welcome bonus was how young it made me feel.

Booster 2. Activate Your Worry WARRIOR

What it's good for: Cultivating resourcefulness

What it is: This powerful practice is designed for you to analyze, reappraise and strategically manage your anxieties. It provides a structured way to confront worries head-on so you can reclaim your mental space by affirming your WARRIOR status (wise, accomplished, resourceful, resilient, insightful, open and reasonable).

What it does: It empowers you to regulate anxiety triggers, mitigate stress, and transform unproductive worry into constructive action.

How to prepare: No preparation needed

How long it takes: 10–15 minutes

What to do:

1. Using a pen and paper or a digital device, list three to five (or more, if others come up as you brainstorm) current worries that are playing on your mind.
2. Stand or sit in a strong, empowering pose (for example, the Wonder Woman stance, with hands on hips and feet apart).
3. Read this statement out loud, ideally to your reflection in a mirror: "I am a WARRIOR—wise, accomplished, resourceful, resilient, insightful, open and reasonable." If a different set of words resonates more deeply, add your own replacements, as long as it still spells out W-A-R-R-I-O-R.
4. Systematically review your worry list using the TRAP framework below:
   - **Truth check** (1–10 scale): For each worry, rate its level of truthfulness in this moment on a scale of 1–10 (1 = not true at all, 10 = completely true).

- **Reality check** (%): Estimate the realistic likelihood of each worry coming true as a percentage (0 to 100 percent).
- **Attention check** (Y/N): Answer yes or no: Does this worry genuinely warrant the attention I'm giving it?
- **Perception check** (healthy/unhealthy): Categorize each worry as either healthy (leading to productive action) or unhealthy (causing unproductive stress) based on your perception of its current impact.

5. Identify concrete steps to address your worries. What will you continue, amend, start or stop doing?

How it works: This booster operates by engaging both physiological and cognitive processes. Amy Cuddy's widely acclaimed 2012 TED Talk, "Your Body Language May Shape Who You Are," featured the concept of "power posing," like taking the Wonder Woman stance, and how it enhances confidence and a sense of strength. While the scientific evidence on its direct physiological impact may be debated, the core idea is simple: If adopting a strong pose makes you feel more like a warrior, it primes you to face your fears with greater courage and conviction.

Worry is a complex cognitive and emotional state, typically characterized by:

- **Negative anticipation:** Focusing on undesirable "what if" scenarios
- **Intrusive thoughts:** Worries often loop persistently
- **Emotional distress:** Feelings of unease, anxiety or fear
- **Physical symptoms:** Muscle tension or restlessness
- **Cognitive biases:** Distorted thinking that overestimates threats

- **Varied reality:** Worries can be realistic or completely irrational

While most people predominantly perceive worry as a negative thing, this booster guides you toward a "healthy" form of it—one that transforms into something productive. Healthy worry is:

- **Problem-focused:** Shifting from dwelling on the emotion to asking, "What can I do about this?"
- **Action-oriented:** Making concrete plans, gathering information, or taking steps to mitigate risks
- **Realistic:** Evaluating likelihood and severity objectively, avoiding catastrophizing
- **Accepting of uncertainty:** Focusing on what you can influence, acknowledging what you cannot

By applying the TRAP framework, you systematically dismantle unhealthy worry and activate productive problem-solving, equipping your inner Worry Warrior with tools for effective action.

How to explore further: Try merging this booster with "Booster 10. Dalai Lama Hakuna Matata" on page 97 to create your own hybrid in a style that suits you best.

How it came to be: I get a tremendous amount out of this booster. Almost every time, what I initially think I'm worrying about is masking what I'm *actually* worried about, which invariably surfaces once I give it the space to reveal itself.

There's a very good reason the weather is often used as a metaphor for the mind. No matter how much time we spend over the course of our lives on self-awareness and becoming better versions of ourselves, every day brings unpredictable "weather." Many people remain firmly domiciled on "Struggle Street," unable to fully accept that is the nature of the world and of being human. This is understandable because it can be frustrating to have zero control over so many things in life!

According to popular psychology, all we ever truly have control over is our attention, choices and actions. Instead of the weather metaphor, I like to think of it as playing the board game Snakes and Ladders (rebranded as Chutes and Ladders in the US); you cannot predict what you'll land on as you roll the dice, or where you'll end up because of it. But isn't the point simply that you continue to play? If you're still on the board, you're winning at life!

Booster 3. Again... and A Gain

What it's good for: Cultivating resilience

What it is: This reflective practice is for gaining insight from recurring experiences and patterns in your life.

What it does: It prompts you to seek deeper meaning and opportunities from situations you repeatedly encounter, turning repetition into a source of wisdom, insight and growth.

How to prepare: No preparation needed

How long it takes: 10–15 minutes

What to do:

1. Start by noticing patterns of similar experiences, situations or dynamics you find yourself drawn to or repeatedly "sucked into." Be specific when you identify the recurring elements.
2. Reflect on the deeper meaning or reason behind this pattern. What opportunity might you be able to gain from this repetition? What could this recurring experience be trying to teach you?
3. Identify any changes you could make. What will you continue, amend, start or stop doing?

How it works: This booster is based on the principle that life presents us with recurring lessons until we truly grasp them. As Soren Gordhamer of the website Wisdom 2.0 would offer: This moment is what it is. So what might it be here to teach me?

While the common adage says lightning never strikes the same place twice, life sometimes seems intent on proving otherwise. By consciously observing these repetitions and seeking the underlying gain or lesson, you move from passively experiencing patterns to actively extracting wisdom from them. This process transforms potential frustration into an opportunity for profound personal growth and resilience. If this time, the scenario is the same as before, or it's at a deeper or more expansive and evolved layer, what is it here to teach you?

How to explore further: If you are comfortable doing so, discuss what's happening with a trusted friend or mentor. Sometimes an outside perspective can illuminate insights you might miss because you're too close to see clearly.

How it came to be: Julia Roberts is a marvel, and her acting is mind-blowingly good. I don't have a particular favorite movie of hers, since there are too many to choose from. Regarding this booster, though, I'm reminded of her character, Maggie, in *Runaway Bride,* and the moment it finally dawns on her that she could decide for herself how she likes her eggs cooked.

Similarly, ever since I was a little girl, I've been "in love with love." Being married three times wasn't anywhere close to what I'd imagined or hoped would happen. My intention was to fall in love and firmly stay there, basking in "happily ever after."

My life would have been remarkably different if the thought had crossed my mind to notice emerging patterns and decipher meaningful ways to develop wisdom, insight or growth from them. Luckily, things turned out better than they might have despite this unintended ignorance on my part, and these days I can count on this booster to teach me lessons from the past, the present, and hopefully prevent me from making choices that lead to any future disastrous walks down the aisle!

Booster 4. Awakening the Buddha Within

What it's good for: Cultivating resourcefulness

What it is: This is an adaptation of a short, guided meditation created by Lama Surya Das, designed to bring you gently into the moment.

What it does: It quiets your mind, promotes relaxation, and fosters a sense of arrival and ease.

How to prepare: Create a recording of yourself slowly reading the words below, allowing natural pauses and ample space in between the lines, or record a loved one reading it for you.

How long it takes: 3–5 minutes

What to do:

1. Settle into a comfortable position.
2. Either close your eyes or soften your gaze (by not specifically focusing on anything).
3. Take a couple of mindful breaths, then simply listen to your recording, gently focusing on either your breathing or the words as they are spoken:

Breathe
Breathe again
Smile
Relax
Arrive
Where you are
Be natural
Open to effortlessness
To being
Rather than doing

Drop everything
Let go
Arrive

How it works: This booster harnesses the power of the spoken word to guide your mind toward a state of present-moment awareness and relaxation. Each short phrase acts as a soothing anchor, encouraging you to release tension, quiet mental chatter, and shift from "doing" mode to a state of "being." By focusing on the simplicity of the breath and the warm invitation of the words, you create a sanctuary for your mind and space for calm to emerge.

How to explore further: If you're new to guided meditations and found this booster beneficial, there's a vast world of recordings for you to discover!

I highly recommend exploring the work of Jon Kabat-Zinn, fondly known as the father of Western mindfulness. His book *Wherever You Go, There You Are* is truly outstanding. I had the good fortune of meeting him briefly in London a few years ago, and I was delighted to discover his warmth and humility are as authentic in real life as they are in his writing.

If you're interested in exploring guided meditations through the lens of Tibetan Buddhism, Lama Surya Das is also an extraordinary writer and guide. His insights are profound, and as a delightful bonus, you'll find when you listen to his recordings that he has the most gorgeous Long Island accent.

How it came to be: I was first introduced to this guided meditation in 2009 by a wonderful trainer, Satyam Veronica Chalmers, who became my mentor, coach, colleague and friend. I've shared this masterpiece widely, and despite the countless times I have said it, *effortlessness* has remained among the top five of my all-time favorite words.

"Live each moment deeply, take each moment lightly" also acts like a soothing balm. By simply bringing this phrase into my conscious awareness, I'm able to generate a positive impact on my mental fitness. The words hold remedial qualities, suspending time as they draw me into a deep state of presence that seems less affected by the ticking of a clock or a looming deadline.

Booster 5. Better Sleep Blueprint

What it's good for: Cultivating resourcefulness

What it is: This is a seasonal, personalized approach to optimizing your sleep.

What it does: It taps into self-awareness to create and maintain healthy, effective sleep habits tailored to you.

How to prepare: No preparation needed

How long it takes: 15–30 minutes

What to do: Answer these questions to guide you to intentionally design a better sleep blueprint:

1. How much sleep do you genuinely need? Use your intuition and be honest with yourself. This isn't about what you currently get, but what you truly require!
2. What is your natural sleep pattern? (For example, do you drift off straight away, or does it take a while? Do you rest through the night or wake up? When are you naturally tired or wide awake?)
3. How are your current routines (your habits and environment) helping or hindering you in getting good sleep?
4. What do you need to start, stop, amend or continue doing to ensure you have created a better sleep blueprint that suits your needs?
5. On a scale of 1–10, how committed are you to prioritizing these changes?

6. What specific barriers are preventing you from achieving what you need?
7. How can these barriers be reduced, mitigated or overcome?
8. Who is the most important person in *your* universe and thoroughly deserving of a good sleep? (Even if you're a parent, I still mean you here.)

How it works: How well do you genuinely understand your patterns and routines? Can you confidently describe what "good sleep" looks like for you? If you're quick to dismiss this question with the assumption that seven to eight hours is sufficient, but challenging to achieve due to a busy lifestyle, then this booster is ideal. It can be highly beneficial to reassess your sleep habits when your body responds to each seasonal change (for example, when winter transitions to spring).

How to explore further: There's so much only *you* can truly know about this essential topic. However, there's plenty of information that applies to the majority of us, and that's an excellent platform on which to build awareness. Sleep research experts, such as Jessica D. Payne, a professor who directs the Sleep, Stress and Memory Lab at the University of Notre Dame, frequently provide useful, readily accessible resources. Understanding how generalized knowledge applies to you, or doesn't, is paramount.

To dig even deeper, use your favorite search engine to discover the superb work of Jessica Payne and Ellen Langer. Their respective contributions and insights into optimizing behavior related to sleep and beyond have significantly affected my quality of life.

How it came to be: In 2011, I met Jessica Payne at the NeuroLeadership Institute summit held in San Francisco. She wouldn't recall meeting me, of that I'm certain, since she was a keynote speaker and I was most definitely a nonplaying character!

However, I've continued to follow her work, and she inspires me. What I learned from her led me to experiment with breaking up the day by sleeping. For a year, I supported my brain by effectively hitting the refresh button, with amazing results. Yet, as a working mother, what I couldn't break away from was a nagging sense of guilt and shame that went with it, and the cruel inner voices screeching, "Living a life of luxury, are we? Shouldn't you be *actually* working? You're so frickin' lazy!"

The relentless clawing was too much to handle, so I dropped the clever sleep habit and went back to sloth-like, less productive afternoons just to shut them up. A few years later, after I learned how to manage my inner world more effectively, I started to practice what I preach by creating my own better sleep blueprint and consistently following it. This transformation led me to become a bona fide "health learner," as Ellen Langer puts it.

I now embrace four stages of sleep within a twenty-four-hour period. The first is a yummy sleep that usually starts around 10 p.m. and lasts four to six hours. The second occurs after a short period of being awake, which I fully embrace and don't stress over, since it's a natural part of my sleep cycle. If it takes a little longer to fall back asleep, I try to remember the layout of the various houses I've lived in throughout my life (twenty-eight so far!). It works brilliantly because it's just the right level of concentration combined with a lack of novelty (no one is there, nothing is happening, it's only walls, floors and windows) for getting me back to sleep.

The third stage is that period between dreaming and full consciousness. Because I'm an extraordinarily vivid dreamer, there's often quite a lot to process from the second sleep cycle. As I've hit perimenopause, I've been experiencing an increase in nightmares, so this third sleep stage is intended to be a peaceful doze during which I can gently let go of the sheer terror that emerged from my subconscious during the night.

The fourth and final stage is the strategic nap in the middle of the day, and it is pure joy. Armed with a silk sleep mask, a weighted blanket, an additional blanket for the dog (who is only allowed on my bed for this nap time), we've honed our routine so well that no alarm is necessary. I wake naturally before going too deeply into sleep and feel refreshed.

While my mood is unpredictable when waking in the morning, after a strategic nap, I always feel cheerful. What's not to like!

Booster 6. Chicken-and-Egg Compassion

What it's good for: Cultivating resilience

What it is: This approach eases suffering by figuring out the best order to offer compassion to someone else and to oneself, much like the classic chicken-or-egg dilemma, based on the context of the situation. Christina Feldman and Willem Kuyken eloquently describe compassion in their notable paper "Compassion in the Landscape of Suffering" as "a multi-textured response to pain, sorrow and anguish. It includes kindness, empathy, generosity and acceptance. The strands of courage, tolerance, equanimity are equally woven into the cloth of compassion."

What it does: It guides you in understanding the dynamics of suffering and deciding whether to offer compassion to yourself or others first for the greatest benefit.

How to prepare: Unless you have an exceptional capacity for compassion that enables you do this in the heat of the moment (in that case, perhaps you're a Buddhist monk), you may need to wait until things cool down before you attempt this booster.

How long it takes: 5–7 minutes

What to do:

1. Determine which of these five poisons is at work—jealousy, pride, anger, ignorance or desire.

2. Identify the source of the poison (you or them) and the target (you or them).
3. Decide what will be most effective: Do you need self-compassion before you can offer compassion to the other party, or are you able to focus on alleviating their suffering first and then address your own?

How it works: This booster prompts you to consider both the source of suffering (the five poisons) and who experiences it as the primary and the secondary recipient. This layered awareness allows for a more strategic application of compassion, either starting with yourself or extending it to others first, depending on the situation.

For this booster to actually work, the intention of compassion, which is to alleviate suffering, must remain at the core of the practice. This isn't about blame. We are all triggered by different things in different ways, and experiencing negative emotions doesn't make us bad people. This is about wanting to address the emotional response experienced as a result of an interaction, no matter what the origin.

How to explore further: Read Kristin Neff's book *Self-Compassion.* If you've already devoured it, check out another marvel, which is Julie Smith's *Why Has Nobody Told Me This Before?*

How it came to be: When I learned about the Tibetan Buddhist concept of the five poisons that drive the cycle of suffering—jealousy, pride, anger, ignorance and desire—it resonated with me deeply. I happened to be reading Kristin Neff's incredible book, which became one of the absolute best and most impactful reads of my life.

This intersection sparked a persistent question for me: If suffering arises from these poisons, whether you're the one acting out of them or on the receiving end, what's the most helpful path forward? I was genuinely baffled by my inability to create a simple model to address this after years of trying. I was fortunate to have an opportunity to approach Kristin with this question during a break at an event she was presenting at in London. But since she didn't have a clear view on it either, I continued to contemplate it, until one day the answer hit me. There's no rigid rule or formula to apply since it will always depend entirely on the context.

Booster 7. Combat Psychic Toxicity

What it's good for: Cultivating resilience

What it is: This deeply personal self-compassion practice contributes directly to your sense of inner comfort.

What it does: It provides gentle, subtle support and protection against negative influences to help elevate your internal energy.

How to prepare: No preparation needed

How long it takes: 2–3 minutes (for initial setup)

What to do:

1. Choose an object, color, image or other item that strongly symbolizes safety, joy, strength or another element that represents something positive for you.
2. Several times a day, take time to connect with your chosen symbol in a way that diverts your attention to promote a positive shift in your energy.

How it works: Psychic toxicity refers to the negative influence certain thoughts, beliefs, emotions or environments can have on us. The accumulation of harmful or draining factors in one's mental or emotional landscape may lead to distress, decreased functioning, and long-term psychological harm.

Examples of psychic toxicity include:

- Persistent negative self-talk, self-criticism or internalized negative beliefs

- Toxic relationships or interactions that drain emotional energy and undermine self-esteem
- Constant exposure to stress, anxiety or conflict in personal or professional settings
- Negative thinking patterns, like rumination, catastrophizing or excessive worry
- Emotional overwhelm, such as unchecked anger, envy or bitterness
- Unhealthy coping mechanisms, like substance abuse or self-harm

By consciously engaging with a positive symbol, you create a subtle yet powerful internal anchor, redirecting your focus and energy away from these draining influences.

How to explore further: Energy *is* everything, everyone and everywhere. If I leave it at that, how might *you* expand your thinking about it? If you truly don't know where to start, check out the Mindsight Institute and "interpersonal neurobiology."

How it came to be: Obsidian is a volcanic glass, and for multiple reasons, it's my rock. It holds a kind of radiant energy that soothes me. So, I have a few pieces of it, including one I've had since 1987, scattered around my home. Whenever I sense a rise in the levels of toxicity directed my way, I discreetly slip a piece into my pocket or clothing and let it work its magic on me.

If you have ever watched the *Twilight Saga* movies, you might recall that the main character, Bella (played by Kristen Stewart), had an unusual superpower that prevented another character from inflicting pain. That's what I imagine obsidian is doing for me when there is conflict in my life or if someone is upset with me.

Most of us genuinely don't want to hurt others, including me. When (not if, and I'm sorry) I do, I find the aftershocks are pretty intense (like someone has made a voodoo doll of me and is sticking pins in it). Obsidian is my way of shielding against those bad vibes.

I combine the physical and energetic protection with an abridged version of a loving-kindness meditation, which enables me to absorb, dissolve and replace the energy I'm receiving with love, care, understanding or empathy, depending on the context. This may sound cheesy, but I strongly believe it's my responsibility to ensure what I'm releasing into the universe is aligned with my values and makes a positive contribution. (I can imagine the eye-rolling when my kids read this someday!)

Booster 8. Coming to Your Senses

What it's good for: Cultivating resourcefulness

What it is: This booster is reminiscent of the classic children's TV show *Sesame Street*, which often announced, "Today's show has been brought to you by the letter __ and by the number __." It's a joyful method of deepening your daily engagement by intentionally connecting your chosen theme to your five physiological senses.

What it does: It helps you tap into your senses to create consistent, positive anchors throughout your day. By infusing everyday moments with representations of your chosen theme, you introduce a subtle yet powerful means to uplift your mood, energy and overall mindset.

How to prepare: Consider setting several random alarms throughout the day to serve as prompts to engage in this practice.

How long it takes: 3–5 minutes, plus whatever follow-up time you determine is needed

What to do:

1. Choose a time frame for your theme, such as a season, a calendar year, or until the next new or full moon.

2. Identify a central or underlying concept, idea or intention that will run throughout your selected period. This theme serves as a unifying element, binding various aspects of your life together, such as one of your core values, a specific change or transformation you're working toward, or a meaningful word or phrase.
3. Select concrete representations of your theme that evoke positivity, energy and enthusiasm across your five senses. For example:
    - **Visual:** a specific color, symbol or image
    - **Audio:** a particular song, sound or genre of music
    - **Touch:** the feel of a favorite fabric, the patting of a pet, the coolness of a smooth stone
    - **Taste:** a delicious, healthy food or drink; a specific spice
    - **Smell:** a fragrant shower gel, a particular laundry detergent, the aroma of freshly cut grass, the scent of a perfume or aftershave
4. Set an alarm or create other gentle reminders to involve these sensory representations in your day intentionally by actively seeking them out. Pause and engage with them at times that best serve you.

How it works: This booster leverages the power of sensory cues and intentionality to reinforce your chosen theme. By consciously associating positive sensations with a central concept, you create a subtle yet pervasive positive influence. Each time you encounter one of your themed sensory cues, it nourishes your mental fitness.

How to explore further: You might naturally gravitate toward specific senses for this booster. An obvious opportunity to take it further is to delve into the remaining senses and see what new insights or feelings emerge. Consider how incorporating a wider range of sensory experiences might enrich your connection to your theme. Why have only one when you can choose to adopt multiple triggers?

How it came to be: Themes are a source of great pleasure for me, so I often have many on the go at once. I wrote *Better* during the Year of the Snake and wore a snake ring on my left thumb as a visual reminder that a snake year symbolizes transformation (connecting to meaning). I love to pause and mindfully take in the aroma of fresh coffee or strawberries because there's nothing quite as good, and I actively seek out the sound of a seagull's cry (connecting to wellbeing). My friend Jeanie taught me to alternate between three to six laundry detergents so the fragrance still "packs a punch" (connecting to resourcefulness). The scent of the sunscreen I buy every year instantly transports me back to Lanzarote in the late nineties, holidaying with my "evil sister" Rachel, and it's as if we were there only last week (connecting to togetherness).

I link all these things, and other intentional triggers, back to the theme of gratitude for a plentiful existence brimming with so many wondrous elements, from clean clothes and fresh fruit to sun-drenched holidays. It fills me with a pure appreciation for this life I'm leading, which is one of fortuitous abundance.

Booster 9. Daily Shamania Practice

What it's good for: Cultivating resourcefulness

What it is: This booster is designed to prepare you for the following day. Inspired by the holistic spirit of shamanic practices, it encourages deep, intentional engagement with your daily life. The term Shamania is a reminder of the key facets of this activity: sleep, hydration, attention, movement, authenticity, nutrition, intention and adjustment.

What it does: It guides you through proactively planning and optimizing important aspects of your life, ensuring you show up more intentionally and resourcefully while remaining adaptable to what surfaces.

How to prepare: Set aside dedicated time to complete this practice.

How long it takes: 10–15 minutes

What to do: Answer these questions to prepare for tomorrow:

1. How many hours of sleep do you need? What time will you go to bed tonight to ensure you get enough sleep? What do you need to do to create a restful environment?
2. What is your hydration goal? What strategies can help you stay hydrated throughout the day and meet that goal?
3. What tasks will require your selective attention? How will you manage distractions to maintain your focus?
4. How much time will you allocate for exercise or physical activity? What type of movement will you engage in?
5. How can you ensure your actions and interactions closely align with your true self? What choices can you make that resonate with your beliefs and values, to foster authenticity?
6. What nutritious meals and supplements will you consume (and within what time frame if you're fasting)? Which foods or drinks will you avoid or limit?
7. What specific intentions will you set to align your thoughts, emotions and actions? How can you remind yourself of these plans throughout the day?
8. What adjustments might need to be made the next day due to how you slept, what mood you woke up in, or any other external conditions that may change overnight?

How it works: This booster acts as a powerful preparatory ritual, shifting your mindset from reactive to proactive. By prompting you to consider these aspects of your daily life before they happen, your prefrontal cortex is activated for planning and foresight, reducing your mental load and decision fatigue. The final step ensures you accommodate any necessary adjustments.

Each of the self-care aspects I've highlighted in this booster is essential to supporting your physical and mental wellbeing:

- **Sleep:** As Matt Walker, author of *Why We Sleep*, states, "Sleep is your superpower!" Prioritizing it directly affects your cognitive function, mood and physical health.
- **Hydration:** Fereydoon Batmanghelidj, author of *Water: For Health, for Healing, for Life* (with the catchy subtitle, *You're Not Sick, You're Thirsty!*), emphasizes the importance of fluid intake, saying, "So many health problems of our society are produced just by dehydration. We can cure many, many diseases, many different things, by adjusting the water intake of the body." Adequate hydration supports every bodily function.
- **Attention:** Psychologist Anne Treisman was a renowned expert in the study of attention and perception. Back in 1969, in her Attenuation Theory, she posited, "The brain cannot deal simultaneously with all the information available to it." In a stroke of genius, she used a cocktail party metaphor to explain selective attention—the brain's ability to tune in and drown out information simultaneously. This highlights the necessity of consciously managing your attention to avoid overwhelm and enhance productivity.
- **Movement:** Regular physical activity is vital for both your physical and mental health, reducing stress, improving mood, and boosting cognitive function.

- **Authenticity:** Aligning your actions with your values reduces cognitive dissonance and promotes a stronger sense of self and integrity.
- **Nutrition:** Fueling your body in the right way directly affects energy levels, mood stability, and cognitive performance. Avoiding what you know isn't good for you also plays a role in your nourishment (which is easier said than done!).
- **Intention:** Setting clear intentions provides a mental roadmap, guiding your thoughts, emotions and actions throughout the day and increasing the likelihood that you'll achieve your desired outcomes while decreasing internal chatter.
- **Adjustment:** Practicing self-compassion builds resourcefulness and resilience and is an essential ingredient for mental fitness. With this step, you are being realistic, flexible and responsive to change, and you can safely avoid beating yourself up over any changes you may find are necessary or fruitful to make.

This intentional review embeds positive habits and prepares you for a focused and fulfilling day.

How to explore further: The questions provided above are a starting point. Within each category, adapt or add your own that resonate with your personal needs and goals—any that would be beneficial to address the day before.

If you have a heightened interest in the physical components, I highly recommend exploring longevity. Peter Diamandis is my go-to source for deeper insights into this field.

Or, if you're leaning toward developing your understanding of emotion, read *The Emotional Life of Your Brain* by Richard Davidson and Sharon Begley.

How it came to be: This booster initially started out with a mainly physical focus, once I had identified that the quality of my days is directly affected by how much sleep I get, how much water I drink, and how active I am. At times when I have nothing whatsoever in the tank, if I can at least take care of these three, then that's winning in my book.

For years, I've desperately yearned to be the well-organized person who prepares as well as possible the night before. Being willing and able are entirely separate things, and so often I fall short. But this practice really helps, because while it addresses important components of life, it also allows for autonomy by asking questions instead of being too prescriptive, and I like that. (So does that pesky inner rebellious teenager of mine who despises being told what to do!)

On the water front (see what I did there), I've noticed a marked, multi-organ improvement since I became an aspiring "gallon-per-day gal." (I'm okay with referring to myself this way because *gal* goes so well with *gallon*, but don't you ever call me that.)

Booster 10. Dalai Lama Hakuna Matata

What it's good for: Cultivating resilience

What it is: This is a playful approach to dealing with life's challenges, blending the Dalai Lama's wisdom on problem-solving with the carefree spirit of the Swahili phrase "Hakuna Matata," popularized by Disney in their '90s-era film *The Lion King*.

What it does: It renews your sense of perspective, reduces worry, and promotes a more pragmatic and less stressful way of approaching difficulties.

How to prepare: No preparation needed

How long it takes: 40–50 seconds

What to do:

1. Read and reflect on these wise words from the Dalai Lama about navigating the ordinary setbacks of life:

    > I call this the "no need, no point" approach to dealing with problems. If a problem has a solution, then it should not be a cause for excessive worry. Rather than feeling overwhelmed, we should simply work with determination to reach the solution. If after careful consideration we conclude that there is no solution to be found, we gain nothing by worrying. Instead, the sooner we accept that the problem cannot be rectified, the easier it will be to carry on with our lives.

2. Now take a moment to hum, sing or whistle the chorus of the upbeat and memorable hit song "Hakuna Matata," as made famous by Sir Elton John. (Want a bit of fun? Check out mentalfitnessforhumans.com/eltonjohn.)

How it works: This booster creates a deliberate cognitive and emotional shift. The Dalai Lama's quote encourages a rational and action-oriented approach to solvable problems and acceptance of unsolvable ones, thereby reducing worry. Following this with lightheartedness injects a sense of ease and perspective, reminding you that even in the face of difficulty, letting go and not dwelling on troubles can be beneficial.

How to explore further: Consider keeping a mental (or physical) list of "problem-solving wisdom" quotes or phrases that resonate with you. You can then pair these with other short, uplifting jingles or reminders that encourage you to shift your emotional state. Experiment with different pairings to find what works best for you in various situations.

How it came to be: I keep a list of some of my favorite song lyrics and quotes from shows on my phone. One that sticks with me comes from *Game of Thrones*, "The Dragon and the Wolf," when Tyrion Lannister (played by Peter Dinklage) gives a laser-sharp response to the heartfelt refusal of Jon Snow (played by Kit Harrington) to swear an oath based on a lie: "That is indeed a problem. The more immediate problem is that we're fucked."

Need I say more? I do love seizing the chance to mix reality with humor in the name of mental fitness.

Booster 11. Discover Your Purpose

What it's good for: Cultivating meaning

What it is: This is a deeply personal investigation into your core essence and guiding principles.

What it does: It goes beyond superficial understanding to unlock a profound connection to your spirit and soul, supporting you in identifying your true purpose.

How to prepare: Block out dedicated, uninterrupted time for this booster, then create a new document on your device or have pen and paper ready.

How long it takes: 30–60 minutes

What to do:

1. Find a comfortable spot where you can minimize interruptions for about an hour.
2. At the top of your page, write the question: "What is my true purpose in life?"
3. Write uncensored, short, sharp answers. Think in bullet points or brief phrases rather than complete sentences, unleashing what wants to surface.
4. Continue writing to get past the obvious conclusions—the ones born out of obligation or those you're inclined to include in case someone else finds your list. Push for deeper, more authentic responses.

5. When you identify "the one"—the answer that truly resonates—give yourself some time to sit with it and absorb its arrival.
6. Decide how this new information provides clarity for what you want to do next.

How it works: This booster is based on a blog post from 2005 by Steve Pavlina, titled "How to Discover Your Life Purpose in About 20 Minutes." My version includes revisions designed to give you more time to percolate and process the insights that surface. The underlying mechanism is simple yet highly effective: By repeatedly asking the question and pushing past superficial answers, you bypass mental blocks and societal expectations, allowing deeper truths from your subconscious to reveal themselves. The extended time frame also encourages a meditative state where authentic self-knowledge can emerge.

How to explore further: If you're looking for inspiration, John Wood's *Leaving Microsoft to Change the World* is a heartwarming account of discovering his calling and taking it to the next level. An important caveat, however, is that monumental change to your personal circumstances isn't the only path to finding meaning. In a subsequent book, *Purpose, Incorporated*, Wood reinforces this by writing, "You don't have to hike high up the Himalayas to meet your purpose." This encourages you to seek direction in your everyday life and smallest contributions, which is significantly less pressure than some grandiose plan.

How it came to be: I've used this booster countless times with coaching clients, and it is such an honor to follow up in a session after someone has experienced this kind of revelation. Often there have been tears, mainly of joy, but sometimes because this feels like truly being seen.

Over the years, clients have used numerous metaphors to explain how it feels, such as a butterfly coming out of its chrysalis or the sun shining through the clouds after a thunderstorm. People sometimes get hung up on their purpose sounding too cliché or cheesy, but I say, "You do you!"

We've collectively conducted this deep inner quest for meaning for centuries. Knowing your vision, purpose and values is the foundation for leading a contented, fulfilling life.

Random side story: I met John Wood in Singapore when he was speaking at an event hosted by Credit Suisse, which is where I was working at the time. After the encounter, I rode the elevator down to the thirtieth floor, but then had an aha moment and ran back up several flights of stairs to offer pro bono coaching for his charity Room to Read. As I burst into the room, completely out of breath, I must have resembled a Himalayan mountain goat with wild eyes! But because I took the leap of faith to align with my purpose, I got to coach an amazing woman from Chicago who was an integral part of his management team as a way of supporting this remarkable charity.

Booster 12. DOnimals

What it's good for: Cultivating resourcefulness

What it is: This is a fun framework to understand and work with your daily energy fluctuations. It recognizes your moods, emotions, cognitive capacity, and behavior are dynamic, much like different animal "modes."

The four DOnimals offer a framework for understanding and responding to your shifting energy:

- **DOdo:** There's a reason they're extinct (or at least they were when I wrote this)! When you're in DOdo mode, you naturally slow down and would likely benefit from a strategic nap or a moment of rest. This is a good time for light duties that don't demand much energy or deep thought, like getting the mail, folding the laundry, or clearing emails from your inbox. Remember, it's essential to recognize these dips in energy and focus are entirely natural—you're a human, not a humanoid!

- **DOnkey:** This DOnimal carries most of the workload. Known for their ability to slog through demanding tasks under challenging conditions, donkeys are problem-solvers, even though they may be a bit stubborn. Stressful environments can destroy their mood and evoke a "don't care, you can't make me" attitude. This is a useful time for focusing on solo projects, unless you specifically want someone's company.
- **DOg:** Dogs are trainable, optimistic and generally pleasant company. They thrive in temperate conditions, though mistakes (like eating socks, chasing cars, or getting hopelessly lost running after a deer) can happen. This is a good time for collaborative work, social interactions, or learning new tricks.
- **DOlphin:** They're known for their intelligence, playfulness, cooperativeness and being highly engaging. When you're in DOlphin mode, the world is your oyster! This is *not* the time for checking emails or mindlessly scrolling through social media. Instead, harness this powerful energy to put toward your most creative, meaningful priorities—the ones that improve your life and beyond!

What it does: It provides a lighthearted, compassionate way to navigate your daily highs and lows. By connecting with these fluctuating energy levels, DOnimals foster awareness and optimize your performance with kindness and self-compassion.

How to prepare: No preparation needed

How long it takes: 3–5 minutes

What to do: Consider how you can best use each of your DOnimal modes today:

1. When is an optimal time of day to channel each DOnimal?
2. What will you do to stay in your preferred mode as long as possible to harness the natural peaks and troughs of your energy?
3. What environment can you create to best support the mode while you're in it?
4. Are there other factors to consider that can help you adapt to today's natural ebbs and flows?

How it works: Elite athletes demonstrate an extraordinary aptitude for balance and discipline. They don't expect peak performance 24/7. Instead, they honor the shifts within an integrated system. That's precisely how this booster works: applying the same logic to reduce friction, thereby creating harmony between your cognitive, emotive, behavioral and energy systems.

How to explore further: If your birth gender is female, you might consider how these fluctuations relate to your menstrual cycle. And for all humans, given that we're predominantly made of water, which is affected by the moon (think about the tides), consider whether your DOnimals are connected to the lunar cycle. Perhaps you're a complete DOdo or become a sleek DOlphin during every full moon, and you just didn't realize it until now.

You can also explore what kind of "bird" you are by reading *Reset Your Inner Clock* by Michael Terman and Ian McMahan.

How it came to be: It's highly entertaining to introduce the DOnimals concept to people because most seem to relate instantly to it and know exactly which mode they're in most days. I tend to start out as a DOlphin, so I like to get underway as quickly as possible, fully aware that my capabilities in the afternoon are severely reduced. Instead of beating myself up about it, my inner DOdo and I do "the slump" stuff (nontaxing tasks) or take that strategic nap. I seesaw between DOg and DOnkey in the midmorning, and I try to step into whatever mode hasn't been featured yet later in the day, when I've regained the capacity to switch away from DOdo mode. Unless I'm massively sleep-deprived, which changes everything, I tend to experience all four modes every day, and it's only the time and duration that are different.

Booster 13. Dynamic Mindfulness

What it's good for: Cultivating resourcefulness

What it is: At its heart, mindfulness is about "being here, not there, and seeing what's here." Dynamic mindfulness takes this a step further by integrating present-moment awareness into the flow of your daily life.

What it does: This booster serves as a continuous reminder to connect with the moment as it unfolds in real time by fully engaging in all you are being and doing.

How to prepare: Gently set an intention to bring awareness to your day as often as possible.

How long it takes: A few seconds, scattered throughout the day

What to do:

1. Without pausing or stopping your current activity, bring awareness and curiosity to it all, and inventory the emotions, thoughts, sensations and actions you are experiencing right now.
2. Repeat this as frequently as you are able to throughout your day.

How it works: While many enriching mindfulness practices (for example, guided meditations and silent retreats) often involve setting aside dedicated time, dynamic mindfulness integrates present-moment awareness directly within your existing environment and activities. It offers an alternative path to increasing your connection to the here and now, since it's about being mindful *in* life, not necessarily taking time *out* of it.

How to explore further: For a simple and succinct reminder, consider using this short mantra, "Be here, not there." This will increase the frequency of your practice.

There are also many excellent resources available to inspire you to build the art and skill of mindfulness. I absolutely loved a great book called *Mindfulness* by Mark Williams and Danny Penman. Trust your intuition and energy to guide you toward resources that equip you to both make sense of and derive meaning from your practice. No one will get inside your mind to judge your experience. This endeavor is deeply personal and unique for each of us—so you do you!

How it came to be: "I don't have time to sit around for an hour a day chanting 'Om'!" That throwaway comment from an acquaintance at a group dinner became a pivotal moment in my self-development journey, permanently altering my path. It landed like fabulous, modern-day wisdom and ultimately sparked the origins of dynamic mindfulness, which I've been practicing and teaching ever since. Life in the twenty-first century can be so full and intense, and the intention behind dynamic mindfulness is to offer a simple, practical and elegant way to stay connected to your lived experience while harnessing an age-old practice designed to help you truly live. These days, "Be here, not there" plays in my consciousness like soft background music, but like a favorite song or melody rather than some form of relentless elevator-music torture.

Booster 14. El Demon-ator

What it's good for: Cultivating togetherness

What it is: This is a playful way to become aware of, and subsequently neutralize, the impact of unintentionally succumbing to the "us versus them" mentality that leads to viewing others negatively.

What it does: It allows you to feel more connected and understanding of people, even those whom you might find challenging.

How to prepare: No preparation needed

How long it takes: 1–2 minutes

What to do:

1. Notice when your negative internal narrative about someone starts up and make a conscious decision to consider a different viewpoint.
2. Think of at least one thing you appreciate, like or admire about that person.
3. Alternatively, identify commonalities—even something basic, such as needing air, water or sleep (the lowest common denominators we all share), is valid.
4. Based on your similarities, take a moment to acknowledge one or more groups you and this person might belong to together.

How it works: Our brains categorize people as friend or foe at an unconscious level. By bringing this hidden bias to your conscious awareness, you gain the power to challenge it. This exercise draws inspiration from Ellen Langer's work on "mindlessness," which encourages finding common ground to prevent the demonizing of others. The "El" in "El Demon-ator" represents her initials, honoring the foundation on which this approach is based.

How to explore further: If you can do this thought exercise with sincerity, take a moment to create positive energy for people simply by sending them pleasant wishes. For example, you might think, "I hope you are having an okay day." To carry it even further, try practicing a Tonglen meditation, which involves cultivating compassion and extending loving-kindness to all beings. Search for the term online, and you will find plenty of resources to guide you through this practice.

How it came to be: In my early thirties, a therapist pointed out my strong tendency toward sibling rivalry, which likely stemmed from being the youngest of two sisters. Their suggestion was that this ingrained, competitive dynamic, which had transformed into deep love and admiration for my sister, might still be coloring my interactions with other women. The ensuing insight was key to recognizing when I developed a "beef" with others I interacted with. Because I have a strong aversion to conflict, this generally remained hidden, even from me, and unresolved. Luckily, it didn't show up very often, and whenever it did, it was predominantly in a professional setting, which lessened its impact.

Nowadays this tendency emerges far less frequently, and thankfully I have the good fortune of having incredibly warm, honest and nurturing friendships with some truly remarkable women. However, it's still a lingering characteristic that arises every now and then and can be particularly intense when it does. This fault is also no longer isolated to women; it's anyone in a similar line of work to mine who I perceive to be disingenuous. For example, the person who claims to have "coached" over 70,000 people, or "mentored" thousands of professionals. What utter bullshit! Or the very senior human resources executive who blatantly lacks emotional intelligence, demonstrated by consistently not turning their video on during meetings.

I find it curious that what people say and do can still trigger me with such ferocity. I make a conscious effort to mitigate the negative energy this creates since it's all occurring within my vibrant inner world and is totally my own fabrication. This is why the "El Demon-ator" is so vital for me. I can't escape being human any more than the next person, and these sorts of traits that lurk in the shadows for each of us need to be carefully managed.

The "I need to eat you" nature of predators is trumped by the "I need to beat you" nature of humans, which would arguably be the most dangerous of the risks we face had we not spent centuries upping the game to "I need to defeat and cheat you." If we can't play nicely and get along now, what on earth will we be like when humans and machines integrate and a whole new hybrid species emerges among us?! Learning to value diversity as a countermeasure to our natural tendency to demonize people will become even more critical than it already is.

That's where the ability to foster togetherness is a worthy superpower. We can absolutely boost our collective mental fitness by cultivating as much connection and belonging as we can muster.

"You did wrong" and "you are wrong" are two very different perspectives. Seeing the contrast between them is a valuable pursuit in the spirit of forming one harmonious, massive, continuously evolving group. I don't see this as yearning for a delusional "happily ever after." It's a worthwhile goal that may result in a better outcome overall.

Booster 15. Extending the Exhale

What it's good for: Cultivating resilience

What it is: This simple breathing technique aids in managing stress.

What it does: It regulates the stress response through its effect on the autonomic nervous system.

How to prepare: No preparation needed

How long it takes: Less than a minute

What to do:

1. Notice your natural breathing rhythm by silently counting the duration of each inhale and each exhale. The exact count doesn't matter, nor does whether they are the same length. Simply observe your breath as it is right now.
2. Gently lengthen your exhale to be one count longer than your inhale. For instance, if your inhale is a count of three, make your exhale a count of four. If your inhale is seven, make your exhale eight. If it feels comfortable, you can gradually extend your exhale even further, but be alert to dizziness, only going as far as remains comfortable.

How it works: The autonomic nervous system comprises the sympathetic (fight-or-flight) and parasympathetic (rest-and-digest) branches. Lengthening your exhale can ease a stress response by signaling to your body that you are safe and not in danger, thus promoting a shift toward the activation of the parasympathetic nervous system to calm things down instead of cranking them up.

How to explore further: Did you like this exercise? There is a complementary meditation technique called a body scan that is also simple and effective. In it, you direct your attention from your toes to your scalp and everywhere in between to bring your focus to your bodily presence. There are plenty of resources online that you can find to explore further. Or try extending the exhale and simultaneously relaxing your jaw or wiggling your toes.

How it came to be: In 2010, I had the privilege of serving as team liaison officer for the Blues, the Auckland-based professional rugby team, when they took part in the inaugural World Rugby Tens tournament in Singapore. The official opening event was held in the elegant ballroom of the Marriott hotel on Orchard Road the evening before the first matches got underway. As we waited for the formalities to begin, I was struck by the palpable nervous energy throughout the room. It was a fascinating contrast to these professional athletes' attempts to appear cool and collected, while obviously feeling jittery on the inside. Sharing my observation and this simple breathing practice with some of the team appeared to bring relief. Their big, broad shoulders visibly relaxed as they learned that the significance of the occasion combined with unfamiliar surroundings was affecting everyone similarly, and that it was entirely normal to feel some level of apprehension. Helping people feel "normal," or at least okay to not be okay, with a technique this simple ought to be taught in schools!

Weirdly, I don't find the act of breathing entirely straightforward and have to be careful with this booster. In 2011, I had a second ectopic pregnancy and hemorrhaged. During the operation, the incredible Gordon Tan had to stop my breathing and put me on a ventilator while, and I have already mentioned I don't use this term lightly, he saved my life. Since then, without rhyme or reason, I experience odd symptoms around what we generally take for granted, since breathing is something we can even do in our sleep!

Apparently, it's an aftereffect of being put on a ventilator and the body needing to "relearn" how to breathe. I've met others who experience it too. (It's always reassuring when your wonkiness isn't just yours after all.)

I'm sharing this story because, while a simple breathing technique may be perceived as a rudimentary exercise, it serves as a reminder that mental fitness and the ways we improve and maintain it are profoundly unique. If you struggle with this booster, firmly placing it in the "too hard" basket sounds like a great idea to me!

Booster 16. Failology

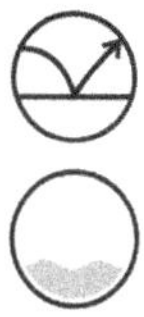

What it's good for: Cultivating resilience

What it is: This approach to skillfully navigating the inevitable experience of failure fosters a mindset of growth and learning.

What it does: Although failure is a natural and recurring part of life, understanding it more deeply can transform its impact on you. This booster introduces the concept of "failology"—a fabricated word representing the pursuit of becoming an expert "failologist," or someone who is adept at extracting value and learning from setbacks.

How to prepare: No preparation needed

How long it takes: 5–6 minutes

What to do: Next time (yes, there'll be a next time) you experience a setback or "fail" at something, consider these words and what they might mean in that specific context:

1. **Fail forward:** An attitude that emphasizes growth and moving ahead, rather than dwelling on the setback. One where *fail* is reframed as "first attempt in learning."
2. **Fail-safe:** An allowance or built-in mechanism that minimizes harm or ensures safety even if a system fails. How can you build a fail-safe into your next attempt?

3. **Fail-fast:** The acceptance that quick, small failures can lead to faster learning and adaptation, helping you move on efficiently.
4. **Fail-ache:** A play on "heartache," this term highlights the very real, often emotional, impact of failure.
5. **Fail-ppetite:** Your appetite for failure. How willing are you to risk, learn and grow by embracing potential setbacks?
6. **Failologist:** Someone who consistently gains more wisdom, insight or opportunity from failing than they lose from it. You, too, can be this person!

How it works: This booster challenges the conventional, often negative, view of failure by introducing a specialized vocabulary to dissect and understand it. By giving distinct names to its different aspects (fail forward, fail-ache, etc.), it encourages you to take a more nuanced and less emotionally charged look at setbacks, which in turn activates your prefrontal cortex, shifting you from a reactive emotional state to a more reflective, problem-solving mindset. The goal is to reframe failure not as an endpoint, but as valuable data and a crucial step in the learning process. This attitude ultimately cultivates greater resilience and an expert "failologist" approach to life's inevitable bumps.

How to explore further: Actively seek stories of people who have experienced significant failures. How did their "fail-ppetite" and "fail forward" attitudes contribute to their eventual success? How do such anecdotes potentially soothe your current discomfort? Elizabeth Day's podcast *How To Fail* is inspiring—part memoir, part manifesto.

How it came to be: My list of failures is quite magnificent. In fact, the two times I recall not failing were in my teens, back in the 1980s, when I passed my driver's license test on my first attempt and was elected as head girl of my high school (similar to being the student body president in many US high schools). Otherwise, I failed exams, boyfriends dumped me, and my part-time job applications were rejected. Failure was a frequent visitor in my teens and beyond.

Around that same time, I experienced my first truly significant failure: I wasn't selected as an exchange student by AFS-International. I was absolutely gutted, not only by the rejection but also because attending the selection weekend meant missing the inaugural Rugby World Cup final in Auckland, where the All Blacks beat France 29–9 at Eden Park. I had to wait another year to reapply for the exchange program, but I was eventually selected and studied in Chile.

I'm now far from being a teenager, and my latest big failure was a professional one. My application to speak at a conference was unsuccessful. Rejection still feels like getting a hundred stings—from bees, nettles, jellyfish and red ants—all at the same time.

One thing holds true though: A loser doesn't fail nearly as much as those who try because a loser isn't trying nearly as hard! Failing is *not* losing by any stretch of the imagination, and this thought genuinely placates me when I consider how hard I've worked across so many arenas: relationships, education, work, health, finance and puppy training, to name but a few.

Booster 17. Formula of Fulfillment

What it's good for: Cultivating meaning

What it is: This is a practical framework for assessing and enhancing your sense of fulfillment in daily life.

What it does: This exercise provides a clear formula to evaluate your activities and identity based on three crucial factors: if you think it matters, if you feel passionate about it, and if it aligns with your core values. This identifies areas in your life where you could experience greater satisfaction, which ultimately produces a deeper sense of fulfillment.

How to prepare: Block out dedicated, uninterrupted time for this exercise, then create a new document or have pen and paper ready.

How long it takes: 60–75 minutes

What to do:

1. Find a comfortable spot where you can minimize interruptions for about an hour.
2. At the top of the page, write the heading: "Inventory of What I'm Doing and Who I'm Being."
3. Categorize your life by the various "hats" you wear (sibling, friend, colleague, parent, etc.) and list what you do within those roles underneath (keep the house clean, plan for birthdays, etc.). You can stay high-level or go into as much detail as you like, but focus on recurring activities.
4. Using the list of activities and roles you created in step 3, ask yourself the following questions:
   - Do I think it matters?
   - Do I feel passionate about it?
   - Is it aligned with my values?
5. Based on your assessment, decide what you will continue, amend, start or stop, and identify anything else you'd like to address as a result.
6. Think about how you might introduce regular checkpoints into your daily routine to reinforce a sense of fulfillment in what you're doing and who you're being. This could be a mental check-in, a quick note, or a moment of appreciation for just being you.

How it works: This booster provides a structured yet flexible approach to understanding and enhancing your personal fulfillment. By identifying all the "doing" and "being" elements in your life, and then explicitly evaluating them against your deeply held values, passions and sense of meaning, you gain unparalleled clarity. The final step of establishing daily checkpoints creates a powerful feedback loop. This systematic reflection transforms abstract notions into actionable insights, making your path to fulfillment intentional and sustainable. It acknowledges that mental fitness isn't accidental but the product of conscious alignment.

How to explore further: Consider this formula, then alter the terminology to make it truly your own. The essence of the exercise lies in the alignment, not necessarily in the exact words. The reason I suggest this is that my lovely friend Beth E. Lee, writer of the brilliant book series *Get What You Want*, passionately dislikes the word *passion*. Once you've designed your bespoke formula, it's useful to revisit it regularly to track shifts in your values and priorities.

To dip more than just your toes into these waters, check out the VIA Institute on Character—it's so, so good! Their material is a super handy reference for identifying your values if they aren't already clear.

How it came to be: I really don't enjoy doing dishes, but I used to absolutely loathe it until I started applying this formula. As a single parent, I could so easily get—and often am—sucked into the 459 other things I need to do each day, and the mere thought of wiping the counter after washing dishes feels like a step too far when I'm exhausted and desperate for bed.

However, while I'm mustering up enough energy to finish whatever tasks are left in the kitchen, it helps immensely if I remember that I think it really matters that our home is spick-and-span because it adds to its comfort. I feel passionate about providing a home for myself and my children that's relaxed and harmonious. These thoughts make it a hell of a lot easier to stomach doing the dishes!

More recently, I learned doing chores also aligns with my values. One of them is humor, and I chuckle to myself as I contemplate that my dish-doing days are numbered. Soon enough, Robert Otway, my humanoid robot, will be performing all these mundane household tasks on my behalf after it carries me up the stairs, tucks me into bed, and lets the dog out for a wee.

Booster 18. Hail-and-Seek

What it's good for: Cultivating wellbeing

What it is: This method provides a way to proactively attune yourself to joy by identifying reliably pleasant everyday experiences, consciously seeking them out, and savoring them when they occur.

What it does: It increases the frequency with which you experience positive emotions, enhances appreciation, and heightens sensory awareness.

How to prepare: Create a short list of three to seven things you find to be enjoyable, such as experiences, activities, people and memories.

How long it takes: A few seconds scattered throughout the day

What to do:

1. Set an intention to seek what's included on your list with a light touch in your approach—like a feather brushing a bubble, not a ravenous person awaiting their food order.
2. As and when you encounter these things, take a breath and indulge yourself in the pleasantness!

How it works: This booster promotes relaxation, activates conscious awareness, and releases dopamine, the reward neurotransmitter associated with pleasure.

How to explore further: Lengthen your list and gamify the seeking element. This could involve using a fun title like "thrill-seeking" or creating a reward for noticing. Alternatively, set an intention to interrupt what you're doing at some point during your day to spend a little more time mindfully savoring your lived experience, leveraging what's on the list you created to act as a trigger for fully connecting to the moment.

How it came to be: A severe case of bronchitis in 2004 resulted in the loss of my sense of taste and smell for over three years, a situation like the COVID-related anosmia many others have experienced. After learning to live with this unseen disability, both senses miraculously returned around six weeks into my sixth pregnancy—I used to tell my son when he was young that he had magically returned my lost senses, as well as giving me a new fondness for, bizarrely, the color yellow.

This emotional journey fostered an immense appreciation for simple sensory pleasures: the smell of fresh coffee, strawberries or cut grass; the clean taste of cucumber, mint or fresh milk—the list goes on. My hail-and-seek list also includes the sound of seagulls, which is one reason I intend to always live near water. Hearing them makes me feel happy and relaxed. And when I catch one of my furry babies—feline or canine—lovingly gazing my way, I try to pause for paws!

Booster 19. Hunch Hunting

What it's good for: Cultivating resourcefulness

What it is: This process shifts awareness from the content of thought to the act of thinking, and then expands into your intuitive senses.

What it does: It enhances mindful awareness and interrupts negative habitual thinking patterns.

How to prepare: Consider setting several random alarms throughout the day to serve as prompts to engage in this practice.

How long it takes: A few brief seconds, though significant insights might lead you down a bunny trail and encourage extended reflection

What to do:

1. Trigger a shift in your attention by turning your head gently to the left or right. Use this simple action to become aware of more than just *what* you're thinking (the content), but *that* you are thinking (the act or process of thought itself).
2. Now that you're aware of both your thoughts and the process, try to access your intuition. What other information, feelings or insights can you bring into your conscious awareness *beyond* your immediate thoughts?
3. Consider the new information or insights that emerge. What does your hunch or gut feeling point toward, and what feels like the most aligned next step to take in response?

How it works: By engaging metacognitive awareness—observing both your thoughts and the act of thinking—you create the conditions for your intuition to be more easily accessed and recognized.

Intuition is a psychological process that involves the ability to understand or know something without conscious reasoning or explicit analysis. It's a way of making judgments or decisions based on information you've obtained from past experiences, unconscious perception, or an innate sense of knowing.

Key characteristics of intuition include:

- **Rapid processing:** Intuitive insights often arise quickly and effortlessly, without involving deliberate analytical thought.
- **Holistic perspective:** Intuition considers multiple factors simultaneously and integrates them into an overall impression or understanding.
- **Emotional influence:** Intuition may involve emotional responses or gut feelings that guide decision-making or judgments.
- **Pattern recognition:** Intuitive insights can result from unconsciously recognizing patterns or connections.
- **Subjective nature:** Intuition is a personal and unique experience that can vary from person to person and across situations.
- **Complementary to rational thinking:** Intuition is not a substitute for logical analysis, but it can complement and enhance it.

How to explore further: Track the trends or patterns that emerge when you're using this booster. For example, notice whether you ruminate more when you're tired, or if dark thoughts point to unprocessed fear. Then, determine appropriate ways to tap more deeply into your indirect thinking, sensing or feeling.

How it came to be: This booster quickly reconnects me to the fact I'm a human, with all the glorious mess that entails. I have a feisty inner drama queen desperately trying to take center stage in an epic tragedy. On most days, she has an insatiable desire to give an award-winning matinee followed by a stellar evening performance. Hunch hunting often aids me in recognizing everything else that is happening—on stage, backstage and in the audience—and allows me to reclaim my role as producer/director. Big feelings can linger like a bad performance, and this practice helps me understand my fear, anxiety, anger and vulnerability. In most cases, that leads to a more self-compassionate reaction. When I avoid emotion, my brain sends me little "ding-ding-ding!" reminders that the show is about to start until I let it play out. I've learned to accept her full theatrical production schedule, which includes rehearsals, a dress rehearsal, an opening night, and inevitably, an encore!

Booster 20. I AMs

What it's good for: Cultivating wellbeing

What it is: This simple yet powerful practice thoughtfully frames your day and guides your focus.

What it does: It encourages you to set your direction with clear *intention*, decide where to focus your *attention*, reaffirms your *motivation*, and leverages your *momentum* for the day ahead.

How to prepare: No preparation needed

How long it takes: 3–5 minutes

What to do: Ask yourself these questions:

1. What is your intention today? (Try letting this come to you with ease rather than forcing it.)
2. What needs your attention today?
3. What is your motivation today?
4. Where is there momentum in your life today?

How it works: This practice proactively creates awareness and encourages you to make conscious decisions about how to approach your day positively. By delving into the four factors of intention, attention, motivation and momentum, you empower yourself to navigate challenges and opportunities with clarity and purpose.

How to explore further: If you especially like the concept of letting your intention find you, I'd highly recommend reading *Big Magic* by the wonderful writer Elizabeth Gilbert. It offers valuable insights into living in harmony with creative energy. To delve deeper into motivation, check out Stage 6 of the Mental Fitness Rocket Booster on page 173.

You can also expand on this by revisiting the A–E of Wellbeing on page 61 or by complementing this with "Booster 8. Coming to Your Senses" on page 91.

How it came to be: I try to do this exercise before I even get out of bed each morning. However, unless I've set an alarm, I often realize when I pour my second cup of coffee that I've forgotten, which is fine. I just do it then.

Despite my experience with postnatal depression, I also have lots of fond memories from living in Singapore, including how my best friend Jen and I would meet at 6 a.m. for "walkie-talkies" before work. Back then, I aimed to set my daily intention in between saying goodbye to her and arriving home—getting into the lift in our condo acted as my trigger.

I have a strong preference for letting my intention reveal itself rather than forcing it. This approach makes me feel like the day and I are in cahoots, completely synced up and working together.

Booster 21. IMBing Mt. Cleverest

What it's good for: Cultivating resilience

What it is: This is an iterative practice where *intention*, *mitigation* and *balance* form the foundation for acting as your most clever self. (Collectively, I refer to these as IMBing.)

What it does: It combines planning with self-compassion to reduce anxiety, foster acceptance of "what is," and deepen your sense of contentment.

How to prepare: No preparation needed

How long it takes: 1–3 minutes the first time each day to anchor your plan, and 20–30 seconds multiple times throughout the day to refocus on it

What to do:

1. Set a clear intention that authentically aligns with your current state—emotionally, mentally, physically and spiritually. Allow for aspirations that are both meaningful and pragmatic.
2. Consider what strategies or tools might be useful to "have up your sleeve" to mitigate the negative effects if you veer off course or are diverted. This prepares you to respond with self-compassion and helpfulness.
3. Reflect on what type of balance serves you best today. Is it linked to how you feel, what you think, or what you do? Everything in moderation.
4. Adjust your intention, mitigation and balance as needed throughout your day to maintain equilibrium.

How it works: Cleverness is directly proportional to simultaneously doing good for yourself and for others. This booster emphasizes intentionally navigating through your day while being fully prepared to be blown off course by a plethora of internal and external detours. The practice then introduces equanimity to maintain a balanced perspective, regardless of your mood and experiences.

How to explore further: The book *Mindful Compassion*, by Paul Gilbert and Choden, is packed with meaningful content linked to all aspects of this booster.

How it came to be: Choden is the coolest monk I've ever met, although I haven't met that many. But even if I had, he'd probably still be the coolest. He was one of my tutors when I was completing my master of science in Studies in Mindfulness at the University of Aberdeen, and years later he continues to be firmly planted in my thoughts, continuously sparking joyful flashes of wisdom.

The greatest lesson he inadvertently (or perhaps intentionally) imparted to me was the possibility of a lighthearted, cheerful form of equanimity, where one can remain in a neutral state in a positive way. I think of it as a subtle leaning toward Swiss chocolate rather than a Swiss Army knife (because Switzerland is neutral, get it?). By that, I mean consciously opting for sweet sensation over function.

I once bumped into Choden in an airport in Spain, and my kids thought it was hilarious. They were quite little and had never witnessed me practically hyperventilate with excitement the way I did—like a Swiftie coming face-to-face with Taylor! And that's not even my favorite Choden story. On a chilly Saturday afternoon in Aberdeen, in a crowded pub, jammed to the rafters with rugby fans watching the All Blacks play South Africa, I laughed my head off as Choden, pint in hand, yelled "Jesus Christ, ref!" at the big screen. Yep, a blaspheming monk! This epitomizes my view of him as an extraordinary human who is as jovial and playful as he is devoted and wise.

One of my mantras for years now has been to "channel Choden," as a reminder to balance lightness with depth to fully *be* in each moment and show up as my authentic self, which means allowing humor and optimism to be omnipresent since they are ingrained into my truest nature. This intent to be aligned with my essence extends beyond the moments when everything is going according to plan. It's perhaps even more crucial—albeit definitely harder—to uphold when I'm tired, grumpy, stressed, distracted, annoyed, overwhelmed or hangry!

I frequently remind myself to live each moment deeply and take each moment lightly, which is what I imagine Choden would encourage with divine enthusiasm.

Booster 22. Insightful Spending Matrix

What it's good for: Cultivating resourcefulness

What it is: This sixteen-square matrix is designed to map your personal resource allocation. It provides a structured framework to visualize how you currently spend your time, energy, attention and money across various life priorities.

What it does: It deepens behavioral awareness by revealing your true priorities and habits in resource distribution. This encourages you to manage and prioritize your finite resources (time, energy, attention, money) effectively and intentionally.

How to prepare: Block out dedicated, uninterrupted time for this exercise and minimize distractions (turn off notifications, find a quiet space, etc.).

How long it takes: 30–45 minutes

What to do:

1. On a piece of paper or a digital device, create a 4x4 grid:
   - Label the horizontal axis with the four categories of your priorities: Need, Love, Like, Want.
   - Label the vertical axis with your four finite resources: Time, Energy, Attention, Money.
2. Consider both labels associated with each square and list the things in it that are appropriate for you. For example, what do you need to spend time on, and what do you want to spend money on?
3. Review the results to identify any patterns or surprises. Consider these questions:

   - Are there any significant discrepancies between where you think your resources go and where they actually go?
   - Are you consistently spending resources on Wants or Likes when your Needs or Loves are being neglected?
   - How might you intentionally shift your resource allocation to better align with your values and long-term goals?
4. Revisit this matrix periodically (for example, quarterly) to track changes in your resource distribution and to notice whether your priorities have shifted.

How it works: Spending is an exchange-driven activity in which we use our resources (time, energy, attention, money) to attain the results we desire. The goal of the Insightful Spending Matrix is to enhance your understanding of how you are allocating these four key elements.

By organizing your current spending habits into the distinct categories of Need, Love, Like and Want, you gain valuable insights into your actual priorities and preferences versus your perceived ones, highlighting areas of misalignment. For example, when you find yourself low in any of the resource categories, this matrix can prompt you to focus more on what you have placed in the Need and Love boxes, ensuring your most vital priorities are met.

How to explore further: "Booster 33. Spending Sanctuary" on page 149 is a good follow-up practice to this one.

How it came to be: I refer to this as my "NeLoLiWa team" and find it enormously helpful in mitigating my strong tendency toward impulsivity. I use my spreadsheet frequently to maintain balance. In terms of financial spending, this booster has saved me all manner of fortunes, from not purchasing a gorgeous but expensive alexandrite ring to not signing up for events I'll never genuinely want to attend on the scheduled day.

If I'm tempted to make an impulsive purchase, glancing at the spreadsheet quickly reminds me of my priorities. My joy and excitement at the prospect of what's included in the Love column powerfully detract from the anticipated dopamine hit of whatever has momentarily grabbed my attention.

Booster 23. Mariana Trench Exploration

What it's good for: Cultivating resourcefulness

What it is: This structured method reduces the impact of mental blocks while simultaneously generating solutions, answers or clear decisions.

What it does: This booster is primarily oriented toward thinking and decision-making, and also lends itself beautifully to an exploration of your emotional world. It activates and leverages your subconscious capabilities to produce valuable insights while alleviating active rumination.

How to prepare: No preparation needed

How long it takes: 5–10 minutes, plus whatever follow-up time you determine is needed

What to do:

1. Succinctly articulate a problem or decision you're facing, framing its resolution as a desired outcome and setting a deadline for when to achieve it. For example: "By 4 p.m. on Thursday, I will have clarity on..."
2. Set an alarm for your chosen date and time, typically 24–72 hours in the future.
3. Block out time in your calendar that will start when your alarm goes off, allocating it to follow-up activities so you can act on the insights that emerge.

4. Try to avoid thinking about the topic until your alarm sounds. If it does creep into your thoughts, consciously stop and redirect your attention.
5. When your alarm goes off, consider what has emerged from your subconscious thoughts and emotions (for example, by journaling, going for a reflective walk, etc.).
6. Leverage the remainder of the time you've allocated to take the next step toward your desired outcome.

How it works: The Mariana Trench is the deepest known part of Earth and serves as a great metaphor for your subconscious brain. It too remains enigmatic and largely unexplored, offering the possibility of potent discoveries.

This booster works on the same principle as the age-old advice to "sleep on it" when faced with a tricky problem or a moment of indecision. But it takes that concept further and creates autonomy by empowering you to choose the exact date and time for your "insight alarm" to go off, essentially acting as a "slow down to speed up" mode of decision-making.

By intentionally deferring active thought, you allow your brain's powerful processing to work in the background, often leading to more creative solutions and less pressure to come up with them. Plus, you allocate time to make progress on your next steps, maximizing the impact of your insights.

How to explore further: For additional reading, there's a fun concept around learning the best time to do everything in *The Power of When* by Michael Breus.

How it came to be: The first time I applied this method, it resulted in enormous productivity and blasted away the procrastination I'd been paralyzed with. I was struggling with one of those tasks at work that seems more daunting than it warranted, so I kept it in the "too hard pile of life" for much longer than was necessary or helpful, and there it lurked in the shadows of my mind, taunting me, until I crystallized the goal, set a deadline, and finally allowed myself to stop thinking about it.

I still vividly remember what happened the day my alarm went off—I'd set it for after lunch on a Friday—and over the next few hours, I worked efficiently and to a surprisingly high standard. It was only a newsletter going out to the team, but that was just over 200 people, and the quality of my work has always mattered to me. So I was thrilled to finish the job before the weekend!

That was way back in 2011, and I still harness my subconscious at every opportunity. It has a deep cleverness that we can all channel when we need it, and we probably need it more often than we realize.

Booster 24. Mind Opera to Mind Oprah

What it's good for: Cultivating resourcefulness

What it is: This transformative method is excellent for reframing challenging internal narratives.

What it does: It regulates mental murmurs that can otherwise feel overwhelming.

How to prepare: No preparation needed

How long it takes: 45–75 minutes to kick-start the process

What to do:

1. Grant yourself permission to be open and curious. See how far you can go with this booster, safe in the knowledge that what you produce is for your eyes only.
2. Listen to your "mind opera." Are there characters who narrate your every move with strong judgments about your thoughts, feelings and actions?
3. Spend some time exploring what you discover by gently encouraging similarities, differences and patterns to emerge.

4. Remain in a self-compassionate frame of mind. These characters are part of you and are probably trying (in their own unique ways) to support you.
5. When you're ready, summon your "Mind Oprah"—the better version of you who epitomizes your vision, purpose and values—and ask what nurturing advice she has for you in this moment.

How it works: If you struggle with a relentless mental murmur that feels consuming and overwhelming, this booster may bring peace by regulating the experience rather than controlling it. There are two key parts to the practice.

The first is to identify the distinct characters who show up in your stories as you go through your day. This may be a work in progress for weeks, months or even years while you gain insight into the rich tapestry of your inner world. Think of it as identifying the key roles in the opera in your head! What does each character symbolize to you? How can they be represented? (For example, can you assign names, images or descriptors for how their voices sound?)

Next, think of Oprah Winfrey. Her journey is a testament to the power of resilience and authentic connection. She rose from humble beginnings to become a global icon, not just through her groundbreaking talk show, but by fostering genuine human connections and inspiring millions to embrace their potential. Beyond her media empire, her unwavering commitment to philanthropy reveals a heart as expansive as her influence.

So, what qualities or figures embody the opposite of your critical inner voices? What "mind Oprah" can you summon to counteract your "mind opera?" It deserves to be the star of the show, the one who is worthy of understanding, affirmation, validation and appreciation.

How to explore further: I'm going to repeat my recommendation to read Kristin Neff's magnificent book *Self-Compassion* to emphasize the importance of treating yourself with respect and tenderness. If you don't, you risk your mind opera transforming into a fully fledged soap opera!

How it came to be: I fondly refer to the characters of my mind opera as "The Seven Sisters," although over time I have identified many more than the seven voices that emerged in the early days. The three main characters, however, have not changed one bit. Their names are Nagatha, Guiltilda and Cruella, and they're... well, ghastly.

Nagatha is constantly hassling me. No matter what I'm doing, she thinks there's something else I *should* be doing. If I'm working, I should be focusing on the kids, and if I'm focusing on the kids, I should be working.

Guiltilda has a slightly different approach. With her, nothing I do is ever enough. Fine, I'm spending time with the kids, but that means we should be having profound, life-altering, bonding experiences. When I'm working, she expects groundbreaking, extraordinary output. In Nagatha's eyes, I'm wrong, and in Guiltilda's, I'm not good enough, so Nagatha is perpetually frustrated while Guiltilda is constantly disappointed.

They both report to Cruella, with whom they share regular updates regarding my inadequacies. She's my stalker, my constant shadow, and always there to dish out venomous cruelty since it's her job to "keep me in my place." These three are the principal singers in my mind opera, but there are many in the chorus.

Maude, for instance, is maudlin without reproach. She wakes up slightly earlier than me, so when I'm shaking off the haze of sleep, I have the pleasure of being greeted by her heavy sigh.

Trixie is a party girl, so she only arises in the midafternoon, and when she does, her number one mission is to trick me into going on strike so I can clock out and binge-watch my latest show. She starts her routine somewhere between 3 and 4 p.m., telling me how hard I've worked and cajoling me toward rewarding my efforts by ensuring there's a glass of something in my hand at 5 p.m. sharp. She's incredibly convincing, making me feel good, and she never worries about my productivity the next day since she sleeps through most of my working hours. If Trixie beats me into submission, it's practically guaranteed Guiltilda and Nagatha will wake me up around 3 a.m. to remind me how foolish I am to get sucked in repeatedly by Trixie's cunning rhetoric.

Out of this "cool gang," Envira will inevitably emerge at some point. She's extremely envious of people who can have one glass and show some restraint. She's also envious of those who don't have a mind opera continuously running, those who are oblivious to what they do to themselves, as well as those that *do* care and show vigilance and self-regulation.

Tyra will then chime in, asking them all to stop since she's just too tired to hear all this for the millionth time. Shakira will vehemently agree because her anxiety is making her feel emotionally shaky, and she's wobbling all over the place.

Oh, and here's Guiltilda again, who has appeared so she can scorn me for oversharing and to assure me that no one wants to hear any of this. And of course Cruella is gleefully chiming in to remind me I'm pathetic and zero people want to read a book authored by a freak like me!

I keep an exquisite handmade wooden box near the desk in my office, and at some point, I will utter "Back in your box, girls" to one or all of my seven sisters and get on with my day. They'll reemerge later because the lid isn't locked (they couldn't breathe if it was), and they instantly grow louder. As the producer/director, my role in this mind opera isn't to eliminate them; it's to shuffle them home when they take up too much of the limelight and don't let me earnestly work toward being a better version of myself.

There's one more sister; her name is Olivia. Named after Olivia Newton-John, her theme song is "Magic." She plays my fairy godmother—my mind Oprah—and I love her deeply. She makes *everything* better.

Booster 25. Nōnification

What it's good for: Cultivating resourcefulness

What it is: This powerful planning tool is designed to enhance productivity and mental clarity, and was inspired by my dear friend Nonie.

What it does: It automates decision-making around repetitive tasks, actively reducing mental noise and freeing up your executive function for high-value activities.

How to prepare: No preparation needed

How long it takes: 45–60 minutes per month

What to do:

1. At the beginning of the month, identify repetitive or recurring small decisions you have to make in your daily life (for example, what to plan for meals and when to schedule appointments and complete routine tasks) by thinking about the next thirty days in minute detail.
2. For each decision, determine whether it can be automated (for example, set a recurring alarm, create a template, predecide specific choices), and if so, develop an automation strategy to declutter your mental activity.
3. Implement this strategy for the upcoming month. (Resist the urge to revisit your decisions and just stick to your plan!)
4. At the end of the month, observe the reduction in your mental load and your increased capacity for more complex thinking.

How it works: Nonie, an avid F1 racing fan, once explained to me her intention to "Toto-ize" her life. Toto Wolff, the principal and CEO of the Mercedes-AMG Petronas Formula One Team, had shared that during the F1 season he limits his decision-making exclusively to F1 matters. He automates all other personal decisions as much as possible, from what he eats each day and at what time to what he packs when he travels. With this for inspiration, I extended the concept to simplify everyday life, and this is how "nōnification" came to be. (This lovely word is a blend of Nonie's name plus "simplification.")

The brain's prefrontal cortex is the master of executive functioning, made up of five clever human capabilities: memorization, inhibition, decision-making, understanding and recall. But since we have a limited amount of glucose and oxygen available to us each day for energy conversion, and decisions deplete that store, this is a truly useful resource for freeing up the finite personal resources you rely on to be as remarkable as you are!

Technology has played an invaluable part in alleviating some of the more mundane, repetitive tasks our predecessors were required to perform. For example, if you're of a certain age, you may still remember frequently used phone numbers you memorized in your early years—if you didn't have a smartphone growing up, your brain was quite magnificent. Now, thanks to technology, your phone can store and recall this information, freeing up your executive function to do other things.

So what can be "nōnified"? Any repetitive decisions, for example, when to mow the lawn, when you'll make that appointment you've been putting off, what time to go to bed, when you wake up, shower, what you eat, whose birthdays are coming up and need to be acknowledged, when to administer flea treatment to furry babies, which day to wash the car... The list goes on.

How to explore further: To dive deeper into the neuroscience behind decision-making and cognitive load, explore the exceptional work of Daniel Kahneman in his book *Thinking, Fast and Slow*. For more on the power of habit formation, check out James Clear's *Atomic Habits*.

How it came to be: At the beginning of every month, I block out time in my calendar for a nōnification hour, during which

I identify how to relieve my poor, overworked brain of as many repetitive or unimportant tasks as possible to make space for better thinking. I include all sorts of things, like deciding when to schedule personal grooming appointments, when to do meal planning and food shopping, which nights I'll allocate for rest or making social plans, which webinars I'll attend and which I'll skip, and so on. When I was diagnosed with ADHD and began to more clearly understand how my brain functions, I finally recognized why this booster is so essential for me.

Ruby Wax explains what a mental bottleneck is and just how much it can limit one's capacity in one of her fabulous books, *Sane New World*. She shares a colorful story about how her days ground to a halt when she developed a fixation on purchasing striped cushions. This occurred long before online shopping enabled us to do relatively quick searches, discover practically perfect solutions, have them delivered almost immediately, and then get on with life. Back then, striped cushions would have been a formidable quest, requiring dedicated time and effort to scour shops in person, with the very real possibility of the outcome being disappointingly adequate at best.

When I read about what I fondly think of as "cushiongate," I too was on an insufferable mission that was preventing me from functioning in practically all other areas of my life. I desperately needed (no, I didn't) a refrigerator with a water dispenser, and until I had completed that purchase and arranged installation, everything was in limbo because my brain was being held hostage!

I was immensely relieved to read Ruby's relatable account because it meant I could finally cut myself some slack. From that experience, a self-compassionate mantra entered my world—"It's not you, it's your brain!" Phew, thank God for that!

Booster 26. Not Fearless, Just Less Fear

What it's good for: Cultivating resilience

What it is: This self-compassion technique is designed to alleviate the powerful stress response caused by fear.

What it does: It loosens the grip fear may have on you through a series of gentle steps that reconnect you to the moment and reveal what else exists alongside fear (for example, love, curiosity, courage).

How to prepare: No preparation needed

How long it takes: A few seconds, and do it often

What to do:

1. Take some time to recognize your fear consciously whenever it arises.
2. With compassionate curiosity, try to identify the source or trigger.
3. Gently acknowledge the fear and its energy.
4. Regulate its impact by consciously smiling through it, even if you can only muster the tiniest of smiles. This small, deliberate act can diminish some of fear's strength by signaling to your brain that you are larger than the emotion you're experiencing and able to manage it.
5. Offer yourself soothing words, repeating phrases such as "It's okay not to be okay" or "My soul's sole home is in the here and now."
6. Try to anchor yourself in the present in whatever way works best (for example, by focusing on your breathing, listening to the sounds around you, or using your other senses).
7. Acknowledge any residual fear that has ventured into the moment with you, doing so with gentle acceptance.

How it works: The world can indeed be a scary place, regardless of who you are or what you do. While this may be a common perspective, it's also accurate to say "Fear keeps us focused on the past or worried about the future," as the esteemed Zen Buddhist monk Thich Nhat Hanh says.

True fearlessness is likely a temporary state, reserved for rare, high-stakes moments and perhaps only experienced by a few, such as F1 drivers or world leaders. Having less fear, however, is far more accessible—and often fortuitous. There are even a few popular, widely recognized acronyms that encourage us to redefine what fear means, including:

- FEAR = feeling excited and ready
- FEAR = false evidence appearing real
- FEAR = face everything and rise
- FEAR = forget everything and run (Ha ha! One of the dumbest things you could do in most situations.)

This booster works by accepting and regulating fear rather than ignoring it or wishing it away. Because our unconscious mind reacts more quickly than our conscious mind can interpret what's happening, we often feel fear before we can rationalize whether it reflects a genuine survival mechanism or merely a habitual hindrance. This makes the pursuit of fearlessness both unrealistic and misguided.

How to explore further: In her book *Radical Acceptance*, Tara Brach offers a wonderful approach to opening our hearts in the face of fear. For a deeper understanding of the science behind being afraid, explore resources available from Robert Sapolsky, who is the legend who wrote *Why Zebras Don't Get Ulcers*, and the marvellous Dean Mobbs, who runs the Caltech Affect Lab.

How it came to be: I once headed into London by train to attend a job interview, feeling sassy and confident that I looked the part in my very fancy Hugo Boss suit. What I hadn't accounted for was the ensuing agony of walking to the station in heels. I'd worked from home for so long that my already wide Kiwi feet had spread out even more. So my first stop at Waterloo Station was at Oliver Bonas to purchase socks to ease the discomfort en route. The closest match to my navy suit was a pair of navy socks with the words "fear" on the left and "less" on the right. I immediately switched them around since "fearless" seems like such a ludicrous proposition, whereas "less fear" sounds idyllic. While I didn't get the job, I still have the socks.

Making the distinction between being fearless—which I certainly am not—and opting to feel less fear is empowering, and this booster has become an essential daily practice for me. The result is that I feel significantly braver than I would have otherwise.

Writing *Better* scared the crap out of me when I started, and throughout this journey, I have clung to the wisdom offered by Joanna Penn in her encouraging book *How to Write Non-Fiction*: "Fear and self-doubt are part of the creative process, and successful writers learn to live with them and create anyway."

Booster 27. OMOlogy

What it's good for: Cultivating resourcefulness

What it is: This is a reflective exercise exploring the personal impact and opportunities within three contemporary psychological concepts: fear of missing out (FOMO), joy of missing out (JOMO), and the fear of being without a mobile phone (nomophobia, or for our purposes, NOMO).

What it does: This booster challenges you to consider your relationship with connectivity, transforming awareness into actionable strategies for enhanced mental fitness and intentional living by leveraging insights from these "OMO" states for your personal benefit.

How to prepare: No preparation needed

How long it takes: 5–6 minutes

What to do:

1. Consider each "OMO": FOMO, JOMO and NOMO. Read the descriptions below to see how each one affects your life.
2. Take a moment to reflect on which ones resonate most with you right now, or what thoughts and feelings each one evokes.
3. If whatever surfaces can be harnessed to your advantage, what might that look like for you today?
4. Based on your reflections, form a mini action plan. What will you continue, amend, start or stop doing as a result?

How it works: This booster operates by bringing subconscious drivers of behavior related to your life into your awareness. By considering how FOMO, JOMO and NOMO influence your activities and attitude, you gain insight into your motivations, anxieties and preferences regarding connection.

Let's look more deeply at what each "OMO" means:

- **FOMO:** This anxiety stems from the perception that others are having more rewarding experiences or opportunities. Recognizing its presence allows you to challenge its influence, potentially leading to making intentional choices rather than reactive ones driven by social comparison.
- **JOMO:** This embraces the pleasure of intentionally opting out of social engagements, overcommitted schedules, and digital interactions. Activating JOMO can foster your sense of contentment, a strong sense of autonomy, and deeper engagement with your chosen activities.

- **NOMO:** This is the anxiety of being without your mobile phone or losing connectivity. Understanding whether and how this affects you can highlight any over-reliance you may have and prompt you to come up with strategies to detach digitally, potentially improving your ability to be present in the moment and reduce your distractibility and stress.

How to explore further: Over the next few days, simply observe when FOMO, JOMO or NOMO arise. To increase your self-awareness, notice the triggers and your internal reactions, as well as how they influence your actions. Pay particular attention to any patterns that emerge.

How it came to be: It seems like the older I get, the more I enjoy solitude. That's probably due to a number of factors, such as historically feeling lonely in the wrong relationships, being able to spend more time alone during COVID, and loving my house and my office so much, just to name a few. So, hearing "JOMO" for the first time (I think the credit for this doozy goes to Anil Dash, a tech entrepreneur and writer) made my heart sing!

At the time, I'd been toying with the idea of creating my first No!vember, an online community event, and JOMO brought my idea to life since I completely relate to the joy of acknowledging when enough is enough and opting out as a healthy alternative. No!vember is all about saying "No!" to things that drain your energy during the month of November to boost your mental fitness.

I have interviewed many people to ask them about the choices they'd make if they could hit a giant pause button on life with zero negative consequences. What would they do instead? (Their answers range from getting shit done to nurturing relationships.) Watching their faces light up as they talk about it is mesmerizing. It seems like we could all use a day, a week, or a month to do more of the stuff that makes our spirits soar and less of the stuff that keeps us busy.

More recently, I was freaked out by nomophobia. I experienced it intensely during a week-long retreat, which was a huge challenge since it was deeply uncomfortable not to be contactable if my children needed me. In their presence, I quite happily switch off my phone for extended periods of time, probably because FOMO is less of a big deal for me. Having spent decades overseas, away from home, I'm used to missing out on birthday dinners, impromptu get-togethers, and the more meaningful stuff, so the fear has dissipated (even if the corresponding sadness will not).

Booster 28. Play Your GAME

What it's good for: Cultivating meaning

What it is: This fun and flexible way to create a personal mantra for big-picture thinking uses an acronym of your choosing.

What it does: It empowers you to tap into and direct your energy effectively.

How to prepare: No preparation needed

How long it takes: 5–6 minutes

What to do:

1. Choose the acronym that best reflects your intentions for today, such as "Great Ascendance Manifesting Empowerment," "Grounded. Aware. Meaningful. Engaged," "Genuine Alignment, Meaningful Existence" or "Gentle Action, Mindful Energy." Or if none of these resonate, create your own GAME acronym that captures today's vibe.
2. Reflect on the acronym you've chosen. While playing the game of life today, how will you embody each of those words in your actions and mindset?

How it works: This booster encourages you to define your approach to the day by consciously creating a personal guiding principle. The acronym GAME serves as a framework to focus your energy on what you deem worthy. By actively engaging with the significance behind each letter, you can cultivate a more intentional and purposeful day.

How to explore further: What other frameworks, such as words or images, could you harness to create valuable daily mantras that will encapsulate your essence?

How it came to be: When I reflect on the lowest points in my life, those times when I wanted the whole world to be swallowed up, I realize how hellish some of those moments were. While boosters like this may appear cringeworthy or even ridiculous to some, it's this kind of personal, word-based approach that consistently prompts me to manage my mental fitness by turning me toward the positives. If I don't actively do it in this way, I'm susceptible to disproportionate emotional reactions. So fuck it! Cringe fest, here we come.

Booster 29. Reappraising Through Another Lens

What it's good for: Cultivating resilience

What it is: This emotion regulation technique is focused on reframing how you perceive a distressing situation.

What it does: It helps you find an alternative perspective on a stressful or upsetting situation, thereby alleviating emotional suffering.

How to prepare: Gently acknowledge the severity of the emotion you're experiencing. Remind yourself it's okay to not be okay. Only when the initial harshness has subsided and you feel ready, move on to the steps.

How long it takes: 1–2 minutes

What to do:

1. Create mental distance by exploring different ways of looking at the situation. Consider shifting your perspective through:
    - **Time:** How will you feel about this situation a year from now? Five years from now?
    - **Detachment:** What would a random stranger neutrally observe in it?
    - **Benefit:** Is there any hidden lesson or opportunity within this challenge?
    - **Context:** Are there other possible explanations for what happened?
    - **Rationality:** What are the facts of the situation, stripped of any emotional interpretation?
    - **Significance:** In the grand scheme of things, how important is this?
    - **Humor:** Can you find anything even slightly amusing about this situation?
2. Check in with yourself to ensure you are genuinely reframing your feelings, not dismissing them. Dismissing emotions is unhelpful and will not manifest the true benefit of emotion regulation.

How it works: This booster, along with other emotion regulation techniques, works by diverting the brain's finite pool of resources (glucose and oxygen) from the reactive limbic system to the rational prefrontal cortex. It achieves this by activating executive functions. You recall what happened, inhibit automatic reactions, actively choose a different perspective, and ultimately understand the situation in a new light. This conscious reframing allows you to manage your emotional response rather than being overwhelmed by it.

How to explore further: Enhance this booster by combining it with other emotion regulation techniques, such as "Booster 31. Savoring the Good Stuff" on page 146, "Booster 38. Venting Feelings" on page 159, and "Booster 41. What It Says on the Tin" on page 165.

How it came to be: One of my long-standing life missions is to be able to reappraise challenges more readily. I'm fully prepared to accept the possibility I'll never reach that goal, but I'll die trying! It's so hard to defuse an emotional bomb, and my inner life is most definitely a glittery, psychedelic, neon rainbow rather than an elegant, sophisticated creamy hue. I do see improvements, however, and I also admit (sheepishly) there's a part of me that enjoys the exquisite intensity of being enraged and completely livid.

Resilience, for me, is all about having an umbrella and not about being able to stop the rain, and I'm less of a drowned rat caught in a downpour than I used to be, thanks to the work of James Gross!

Humor has provided me with protection from these torrents since I first began focusing on resilience, and creating outrageous statements is a favorite tactic. I will construct a sentence starting with, "It's as if..." and pair it with a ridiculous ending, like "... everyone's out to get me." There's something about being that ludicrous that tickles me, calming me down instantly.

I adore these words from Iona David's engaging book, *Is This Love or Dopamine?*, which beautifully demonstrates the use of humor as an emotion regulation technique:

> Love can be really difficult. Sometimes it can be traumatic; sometimes it can fuck us up and make us wonder if we'll ever get over it. There is so much important material out there about how to heal yourself from these things, and there is so much internal work that we all have to do—but, also, you can give your lovely self a break sometimes, and take a moment to laugh at the sheer absurdity of it all.

What *not* to do: Here's a super important caveat. Please resist the very natural temptation to apply this booster or any other form of reappraisal to someone else's emotion. You cannot and should not *ever* attempt to do so on behalf of another. It's dismissive at best and can be irreversibly damaging to your relationship at worst. It is also completely lacking in what it means to show true compassion. I beg of you—if you genuinely want to alleviate someone else's suffering—listening is a far more effective alternative.

Booster 30. SAS Checklist

What it's good for: Cultivating resourcefulness

What it is: This is a fun yet effective exercise designed to bring clarity and focus to your to-do list.

What it does: It motivates you by dangling a tempting carrot—the reward of feeling "smug as shit" (SAS)—to increase your focused attention on and drive toward completing the day's key tasks.

How to prepare: No preparation needed

How long it takes: 2–3 minutes

What to do:

1. Identify the tasks, activities or behaviors that, if you were to complete them today, would make you feel smug as shit. Be specific and realistic, aiming for a list that feels achievable yet utterly satisfying.
2. Work toward ticking everything off your SAS checklist throughout the day.
3. At bedtime, if you've finished everything, bask in that smug feeling to your heart's content!

How it works: This booster taps into intrinsic motivation through several principles. First, it offers autonomy by allowing you to choose how to measure the day's success, aligning with tasks that genuinely resonate with you. Second, by clearly identifying key accomplishments upfront, it focuses your attention and directs your energy toward what truly matters.

Finally, the smug-as-shit reward isn't just a quirky phrase; it's a potent trigger for your brain's reward system, releasing dopamine. This positive reinforcement strengthens the neural pathways associated with achievement, making you more likely to repeat successful behaviors in the future. It transforms task completion from a chore into a highly gratifying experience—winning at life!

How to explore further: Experiment with making your SAS list slightly more ambitious on high-energy days, and intentionally shorter and more manageable on low-energy days. Ultimately, your goal is to accumulate frequent wins. On Arianna Huffington's Thrive Global website, there are some excellent blog posts about this, referred to as "microsteps."

How it came to be: I really enjoy doing this because my days vary quite a lot in terms of my mood and motivation. So, when I'm at a low ebb, the opportunity to feel good about something at the end of the day—even if it's just feeding the animals and drinking enough water—is packed with self-kindness. On high-energy days, the checklist naturally becomes much longer and more detailed. Purely for self-amusement, I add a touch of flavor by referring to my checklist items as *piccoli passi*, which is Italian for "baby steps." It has a lovely, cheerful ring, making tasks sound way more appealing and special.

Booster 31. Savoring the Good Stuff

What it's good for: Cultivating resourcefulness

What it is: This is a simple yet powerful practice that uses your photo collection intentionally to evoke and extend positive emotions.

What it does: It consciously accesses and intensifies your feelings of joy, love, contentment and appreciation, providing a quick and accessible way to lift your mood.

How to prepare: No preparation needed, apart from grabbing your phone (assuming that's where your photos are stored) or a photo album.

How long it takes: 2–5 minutes

What to do:

1. Set an alarm for two to five minutes, depending on how much time you have available.
2. Review your photos and randomly select one that naturally makes you feel good. It might be of a loved one, a cherished experience, or a beautiful place.
3. As you look at it, intentionally invite and encourage positive emotions. When negative thoughts emerge (which is a normal brain function, not a personal failing), gently acknowledge them and let them pass, redirect your focus back to the positive feelings, and proactively welcome more.
4. Pay attention to the physical feelings attached to these positive emotions. Do you feel a smile forming? A sense of warmth or joy in your chest?
5. Notice your breathing. Has it quickened, slowed or remained the same?
6. Continue randomly selecting photos, repeating the process until your alarm signals the end of your savoring practice.

How it works: This booster leverages the power of visual cues and intentional focus to engage your brain's positive emotional circuitry. By actively choosing a photo that evokes nourishing feelings and consciously dwelling on those sensations, you interrupt negative thought patterns and train your mind to sustain positive effects. Paying mindful attention to pleasant experiences enhances their emotional impact and can create a lasting affirmative residue, building your resilience and capacity for joy.

How to explore further: Enhance this booster by combining it with other emotion regulation techniques, such as "Booster 29. Reappraising Through Another Lens" on page 141, "Booster 38. Venting Feelings" on page 159, and "Booster 41. What It Says on the Tin" on page 165.

How it came to be: I've facilitated this practice countless times in workshops and during individual coaching sessions, and it's always so nice to observe the warmth and positivity it generates! Love is all around us, and yet our lives get swamped with minutiae, deadlines and worries. I leap at any opportunity to take a moment to savor the huge pool of love and connection I have to deeply enrich my day.

Booster 32. Sōl Searching

What it's good for: Cultivating resourcefulness

What it is: This quick and zesty reflective practice reminds you of your inherent significance and encourages you to place yourself at the center of your universe—just as every other living creature occupies the center of theirs.

What it does: It affirms your unique place in the world, fostering a sense of self-worth and purpose without veering into arrogance or narcissism.

How to prepare: No preparation needed

How long it takes: 2–3 minutes

What to do:

1. Take a moment to review these positive words, which all begin with "sol": solitude, solace, solidarity, solidify, solicitude, solution, solve, solstice, solid, sole, solar and solo.
2. *Sōl* is Latin for "sun"—the primary energy source for all life. You are simultaneously a recipient of it and the main source of energy for your own life. Take a moment to contemplate your fundamental connection to this external, life-giving force, and your equally powerful internal one.
3. Which word or words from the list stand out for you and serve as a potent reminder of your abundant energy and significance today?
4. Reflect on *why* those words resonate with you in this moment.

How it works: This booster taps into a profound sense of personal agency and inherent worth. It shifts your perspective from being a peripheral player in the world to recognizing yourself as the central sun of your own existence.

The concept is underscored by a wisdom often attributed to Ernest Hemingway: "There is nothing noble about being superior to your fellow man; true nobility means being superior to one's former self." This perspective encourages self-improvement not as a competitive act against others, but as an internal journey of growth, with you as the primary focus and driver. By connecting to the symbolic power of the sun and reflecting on words that affirm your core being, you strengthen your internal locus of control and nurture your inner energy source.

How to explore further: Spend time outdoors, consciously connecting with the sun's energy, and reflect on its role as the ultimate source of life, mirroring your own personal power.

How it came to be: My continual delight in wordsmithing has entertained me over the years. I turn many of my creations into little songs in my head, and my kids often catch me singing them out loud at home. It's never pretty, because they're basically awful and not fit other than for feline and canine ears. On the day I put this booster into words, the lyrics were particularly dreadful: "Let your soul find your sōl church / but don't be an arsehole during your search."

I can't really be held accountable; it's just how my weird brain rolls. For example, one time I had a good old chuckle with the vet after pointing out the bizarreness of the sentence, "Dogs don't have feet." I am sure most people would not find this so absurdly funny.

Booster 33. Spending Sanctuary

What it's good for: Cultivating resourcefulness

What it is: This practice leverages the dual meaning of the word "sanction"—both to permit and to forbid—so you can establish a "sanctuary" for your finite resources.

What it does: This booster supports you in setting intentional boundaries and making deliberate choices about how you spend your time, energy, attention and money, protecting them from unintended leaks or diversions and ensuring your decisions align with your true priorities and values.

How to prepare: Complete "Booster 22. Insightful Spending Matrix" on page 124.

How long it takes: 5–10 minutes

What to do:

1. Revisit your completed Insightful Spending Matrix.

2. Identify vulnerabilities by asking yourself:
    - Where does my spending (of time, energy, attention or money) most often spiral out of control?
    - In which categories (Need, Love, Like, Want) or resources (Time, Energy, Attention, Money) am I most susceptible to being drawn off-track?
    - What will you allow more of? (For example, "I sanction myself to spend thirty minutes of attention daily on creative hobbies.")
    - What will you restrict or limit? (For example, "I sanction myself from spending more than one hour of energy on unproductive social media scrolling.")
3. Decide which sanctions you want to establish based on your insights. What do you want to permit moving forward, and what do you want to forbid?

How it works: This booster challenges you to think about the often-unconscious ways you use up your resources. Your thoughts might automatically jump to money, but you have others that are also finite! This exercise prompts you to contemplate this question across all the categories identified in your Insightful Spending Matrix.

By applying sanctions, that is, the rules instigated and enforced *by you, for you,* you can take back control. This process empowers you to choose what to permit (to nurture growth and alignment with values) and what to forbid (to prevent depletion and distraction). This deliberate self-governance aligns your actual daily resource distribution with your highest priorities, moving from reactive spending to intentional management.

How to explore further: Consider tracking how well you adhere to your sanctions for a week. What insights do you gain? Where are the persistent leaks, and what might be causing them?

How it came to be: There is a statue outside the National Archives in Washington, DC, called *Guardianship* that was created by James Earl Fraser in 1935. Inscribed on its pedestal is the quote: "Eternal vigilance is the price of liberty."

This phrase didn't make sense to me when I first stumbled upon it in Craig Hassed's excellent book *Know Thyself.* However, once I did understand it, it seemed applicable to practically everything. Human existence all revolves around balance. And in order to gain autonomy regarding what needs balance in your own life, it requires paying constant attention to the many facets of living.

The issue I face with vigilance is that if a situation compromises my sovereignty too much, my inner teenager rebels. For instance, if a friend says, "You should go," after I've complained about having plans when I actually want to chill at home, hearing "should" almost certainly guarantees I'll make my excuses and head for a comfy night on my sofa, fully embracing JOMO.

Similarly, when the wise, clever part of me advises an early night, yet again, my inner teenager has other ideas. I end up scrolling through funny cat/dog posts for hours instead. So this booster is particularly tricky for me to adhere to, and the challenge definitely lies with me, not the practice!

Booster 34. Surf's Up

What it's good for: Cultivating meaning

What it is: This booster's name uses a memorable homophone as a reminder for the acronym "CERF," which stands for contented, energized, relaxed and fulfilled. It is designed to connect you with what feels truly meaningful to you today.

What it does: It encourages you to take a bird's-eye view of three controllable factors—attention, choice and action—along with energy management.

How to prepare: No preparation needed

How long it takes: 1–2 minutes

What to do: As you start your day, answer these questions with total honesty:

1. What brings contentment to your life today?
2. What do you need to be energized about today?
3. What do you need to be relaxed about today?
4. What brings fulfillment to your life today?

How it works: This booster encourages you to explore your lived experience more deeply by focusing on the four key elements of contented, energized, relaxed and fulfilled that give you a clearer understanding of what constitutes a good energetic balance and feels meaningful to you.

How to explore further: Ask yourself these questions every day for a while, such as a week, a month, a year, or even longer if that could be of value. If *happy* is a word that sits well with you, you could try swapping the first two questions with "What will make you happy today?" and use the acronym HER (Happy, Energized, Relaxed) to remind yourself what this booster means.

How it came to be: When I think of the words *contentment* and *fulfillment*, the idea that they are worthwhile pursuits, even on shitty, unhappy days, resonates deeply with me. I have a vivid memory of a friend remarking over dinner that I looked content, which I genuinely was at that time. It struck me as such a warm and wonderful compliment, and that word has held significant meaning for me ever since. You'll find more information on creating fulfillment in "Booster 17. Formula of Fulfillment" on page 113.

If I can progress toward any of these states, I feel closest to the better version of myself I aspire to embody. So, I repeat to myself, "CERF's up!" "CERFer dude," or "CERFing safari." These horrifically cheesy phrases encourage me to navigate each day as positively as possible, while sparing me the enormous pressure of having to be happy.

Booster 35. The F Model

What it's good for: Cultivating resourcefulness

What it is: This autonomous schema for productivity encompasses three key elements: focused attention, fixed time, and following energy.

What it does: It optimizes performance by aligning your tasks with your natural energy fluctuations.

How to prepare: Have your to-do list and an alarm ready.

How long it takes: Flexible duration

What to do:

1. Review your current to-do list.
2. Instead of determining what to do by priority level, select a task based on your energy—what are you most drawn to doing in this moment?
3. Set a timer for a duration beginning with the letter "F" that most closely aligns with the level of energy you have available (for example, four, fifteen, forty or fifty-nine minutes).
4. Switch off notifications and make a deal with yourself to apply your focused attention to the task at hand for the duration you've chosen, ignoring all distractions.
5. When the alarm sounds, stop. Or if you're on a roll, carry on!

How it works: This method sharpens your attention for a fixed period, empowering you to follow your energy rather than forcing it. It also leverages intrinsic motivation by giving you control over *what* you focus on and for *how long*, optimizing your natural productivity rhythms.

How to explore further: To delve into the relationship between stress and performance, search online for information about the Yerkes-Dodson law (created in 1908–1909) and consider how it relates to your own optimal operating state. Or, if you want to go deeper, Daniel Goleman's book *Focus* is a real gem when it comes to learning about attention spans.

How it came to be: In 2012, I was *not* awarded a postgraduate certificate in the Neuroscience of Leadership, since I failed the research project twice. The F Model was the subject of said research project, and I still use what I discovered to this day. This failure was entirely due to my lack of skills as a researcher and had nothing to do with the effectiveness of the F Model itself!

Often, I'm asked about the similarities between the F Model and other time management methods, like the Pomodoro technique. The F Model offers more autonomy through the selection from a wide range of finite durations, each starting with the letter "F," beginning with four minutes and increasing to fifty-nine minutes. In addition, being able to follow your energy provides a valuable sense of autonomy and control, which can be incredibly empowering and motivating.

In the second attempt of my failed research project, the results provided statistically significant evidence of the effectiveness of this approach in focusing one's attention. So while the F Model delivered, its researcher (moi!) spectacularly botched the presentation of those findings.

If you've seen the 2017 remake of the movie *Jumanji*, do you remember how the characters hit their chests to reveal a pop-up showing their strengths and weaknesses? My weakness list would include, in no particular order, the inability to apply research methodologies robustly, my lack of aptitude for remembering sports results, and an insatiable fondness for chocolate.

Booster 36. The Iceberg-to-Salzberg Shift

What it's good for: Cultivating wellbeing

What it is: This booster, inspired by Sharon Salzberg, is designed to counteract your inner critic and nurture self-love. It gently shifts the focus from the chill of hidden negativity to the warmth of openhearted kindness.

What it does: This exercise combats your natural negativity bias and quiets your critical inner voice by introducing a deeply nurturing and nourishing reminder of self-kindness and acceptance.

How to prepare: No preparation needed

How long it takes: 2–3 minutes

What to do:

1. Read this excerpt from Sharon Salzberg's beautiful, bestselling book *Real Love* aloud to yourself:

   > Real love allows for failure and suffering. All of us have made mistakes, and some of those mistakes were consequential, but you can find a way to relate to them with kindness. No matter what troubles have befallen you or what difficulties you have caused yourself or others, with love for yourself you can change, grow, make amends, and learn. Real love is not about letting yourself off the hook. Real love does not encourage you to ignore your problems or deny your mistakes and imperfections. You see them clearly and still opt to love.

2. After reading, take a moment to consider what "opting to love" yourself looks like for you today, in your current circumstances.

How it works: This booster intentionally introduces a compassionate narrative that directly challenges common patterns of self-criticism. The text, so beautifully written by Sharon Salzberg, serves as an affirmation, guiding your mind away from harsh self-judgment and toward a more accepting and growth-oriented perspective. By consciously choosing to love yourself, even amid imperfections or past mistakes, you activate pathways for kindness and resilience, fostering a more supportive internal environment for mental fitness. It's a deliberate act to replace a chillingly critical "iceberg" of hidden harshness with the nurturing flow of "Salzberg" compassion.

How to explore further: Delve into Sharon Salzberg's extensive work in any format you prefer—books, talks or guided meditations (she generously shares much of her wisdom online)—and allow her transformative teachings to touch your heart. Her insights are a rich source for deepening self-compassion and understanding real love.

You can also expand on this by revisiting the A–E of Wellbeing on page 61.

How it came to be: I vividly recall an intense discussion with a friend, during which she proposed I suffered from "self-loathing," a term I was unfamiliar with at the time. I was horrified by the thought and deeply hurt by her apparent misunderstanding of my nature. The friendship ran its course soon after, but my inquisitive mind lingered on what it might truly mean to loathe oneself, and what it might look like from the outside to observe, or at least assume, this trait in someone.

What I have come to conclude, based on my limited understanding of what self-loathing means, is that I could never truly hate myself, just as I couldn't feel that way about anyone else. I might be annoyed, irritated, disappointed or even disgusted by someone's thoughts or behavior (mine included), but that word brushes up against an inbuilt boundary I can't and won't cross. Words carry enormous context for me, and I'm still trying to fathom my disdain for this one.

Booster 37. Uncompsciously Screwing with You

What it's good for: Cultivating resilience

What it is: This tactical practice is designed to illuminate the subconscious thoughts and emotions that subtly drive your behavior.

What it does: It uncovers invisible influences that may be inadvertently shaping your thoughts, feelings and actions, and enables you to recognize the subtle ways your mind might be working against your conscious intentions. (Note that the title of this booster is a play on its hidden comparing and competing aspects.)

How to prepare: Block out dedicated, uninterrupted time for this exercise and minimize distractions (turn off notifications, find a quiet space, etc.).

How long it takes: 15–20 minutes

What to do:

1. Expand your focus from simply thinking to thinking about your extraordinary human ability to think—a practice known as metacognitive awareness. Temporarily aim for a broader, objective helicopter view of your mental landscape.
2. From this elevated perspective, consider these words one at a time for a moment or two to see what might stand out: compete, compare, compound, compress, compensate, compromise and complicate.
3. Without harshness or being overly critical (you are human, after all), try to identify whether any of these words represent something inadvertently affecting your current thoughts, feelings or behavior.
4. Consider how these dynamics might be at play beneath your conscious awareness and may even be undermining you at times.

How it works: This booster draws from the rich research in Bob Kegan and Lisa Lahey's groundbreaking bestseller *Immunity to Change*, combined with Luke Burgis's insightful coverage of mimetic theory in *Wanting*. Many of our actions stem from unconscious comparisons and internal competing commitments, often fueled by mimetic desire: the tendency to want what others want. By looking at these hidden forces through a kaleidoscope of different words, you shine a light on them, making the unconscious conscious and creating a landscape where you can have more autonomy over your choices and intentions.

How to explore further: The primary purpose of this booster is simply to raise your awareness around how your feelings, thoughts and behavior are not always as straightforward as they seem. However, if you feel ready to take a deeper dive and can do so safely cocooned in self-compassion, you could extend this practice by considering the panopticon effect. This refers to a social and psychological phenomenon where individuals modify their behavior and self-regulate because they believe they might be being watched. What does potentially being under constant observation or even scrutiny (for example, through being online) manifest that may misalign with internal competing commitments? What might you continue, amend, start or stop doing?

How it came to be: One of the strangest words I've ever encountered is "comptroller"—someone who oversees accounts—and when I first heard it, I thought it was a mistake. You may have experienced something similar with the title for this booster. Apologies for any discompfort (ha ha, see what I did there?) it caused. It is a quirk of the English language that the *comp* beginning of many words shares its root with the *com* prefix—both meaning "with," "together with," or "in combination." I find this a fairly comrehensive (did it again, I kill me!) list of what might bubble up from beneath the surface, shielding us from the truth we're seeking about why we sometimes do the crazy things we do. But you could end up adding other words as you peel apart this tasty little onion, and they don't all have to begin with "comp" or even "com" for that matter!

Booster 38. Venting Feelings

What it's good for: Cultivating resilience

What it is: This is one of the most powerful emotion regulation tools, especially when practiced with conscious intention and awareness.

What it does: It enables the release of pent-up emotions, alleviates emotional tension, avoids the unhealthy suppression of feelings, and relieves internal pressure or stress.

How to prepare: No preparation needed, though choosing a private and safe space is key—somewhere you can be confident you won't be overheard, such as driving alone, showering or walking the dog.

How long it takes: 20–30 seconds, or longer if you love this one

What to do:

1. Vocalize any strong negative emotions you may have through brief, intense and uncensored statements that stem directly from your feelings. These expressions don't need to be rational or diluted in any way. Instead, enable the raw emotion you're experiencing to find an unfiltered outlet.
2. Notice whether or not you feel a difference afterward.

How it works: Vocalizing strong emotions, even briefly, can alleviate the physiological arousal associated with those feelings. This process can provide a temporary release and prevent emotions from becoming trapped and intensified within the body. The act of giving voice to the feeling, without needing elaborate explanation, can be cathartic.

How to explore further: Enhance this booster by combining it with other emotion regulation techniques, such as "Booster 29. Reappraising Through Another Lens" on page 141, "Booster 31. Savoring the Good Stuff" on page 146, and "Booster 41. What It Says on the Tin" on page 165.

How it came to be: I've been blessed with a no-holds-barred kind of friendship where we intentionally vent to one another within a "circle of trust." This is a significant source of comfort and validation for us both. We're aware venting can quickly devolve into unproductive bitching and moaning, becoming toxic if unchecked. So we consciously enter this metaphorical circle for the rapid release of intense feelings in a safe space. It acts as a pressure valve rather than a continuous outpouring, invariably involves lots of swearing and eye-rolling, and often culminates in laughter as we amuse ourselves with expletives and unbridled, wild emotion. In my opinion, everyone needs a friend like that, and I'm so grateful to have such a special one.

Booster 39. Watch Your WATCH List

What it's good for: Cultivating togetherness

What it is: This proactive method and planning tool encourages you to manage external influences consciously by using a "discern and discard" approach to ensure alignment with your values.

What it does: This booster enhances your autonomy by proactively preventing the absorption of rhetoric or behaviors that are not aligned with your core values. Consciously discerning who or what influences in a personalized WATCH list (Who Are The Coolest Humans), you may also foster a stronger sense of connectedness with individuals or groups that resonate with your values.

How to prepare: Complete "Booster 17. Formula of Fulfillment" on page 113.

How long it takes: 20–30 minutes, repeated regularly (for example, weekly, monthly, quarterly, or semi-annually) to maintain relevance

What to do:

1. Reflect on the core values you identified in the Formula of Fulfillment booster.
2. Evaluate your recent thoughts, feelings and behaviors to spot opportunities where you can realign with those values.
3. Remind yourself this is not intended to be an exercise that evokes feelings of guilt or shame! It is simply a chance to tweak your course, if needed, toward a value-oriented approach to living.
4. With openness and curiosity, identify individuals who are currently conducting themselves according to a clear set of values (even if theirs aren't fully aligned with yours).
5. Create a WATCH list of five to ten people to observe casually between now and the next time you do this booster, with the intent to draw positive inspiration from them.

How it works: Online algorithms create exceptionally powerful information streams that influence us more than we realize. By continuously updating your WATCH list, you are actively retaining control by discerning the information's value and discarding what is not serving you.

Combining this mindful selectivity with a clear values orientation enables you to stay on top of a rapidly changing world.

How to explore further: There is so much great content to discover, and I recommend deepening your understanding of influence through the lens of vulnerability. This may reveal to you why your perspectives are shaped by certain people more than others, whether that's positively or negatively. Any work by Brené Brown is pure gold, and one of my favorite books of hers is *Daring Greatly*, which I think adds an excellent foundation to this booster.

How it came to be: Having had plenty of coaching and therapy, I'm still sometimes gobsmacked by how stubborn my ignorance can be, so I'm well aware of how this practice is worthwhile yet very challenging! We are inundated with information, and on top of that, we're incredibly impressionable. That results in making assumptions and conclusions that lack the depth of context.

There are so many extraordinary people doing good in the world that we can grow and learn from, and yet those lessons are all too easily obscured when we become judgmental toward others, turning our attention in the opposite direction of what may truly align and support our evolution.

I agree wholeheartedly with Brené's statement in her book *Daring Greatly* that "judgment exacerbates disconnection." I sheepishly admit that, despite working on this for years, I default to being "judgy" about people and things many times a day, and it drives me nuts. This is why it's super important to address my ugliness with kindness; there's a very vulnerable part of me trying to protect, prove and prevent.

The groundbreaking work of Tasha Eurich, a global authority on self-awareness, offers a powerful pivot. In her book *Shatterproof*, confidence, choice and connection are identified as the meta-skills required to thrive—a soothing antidote to the friction of judgment!

Years ago, in a stress management training program I was delivering in Singapore, I initiated debates with a controversial statement: I asserted that the moon is made of cheese and then encouraged participants to challenge me on my outlandish assertion. Super fun! The point was to show how attached we get to our beliefs, long after we've been influenced by whoever educated us into agreeing with their perspective. This has become exceptionally dangerous territory now that we have so much information at our fingertips that might not come from a trustworthy, validated and verified source.

What a tricky business it is to know what to believe, and it's not isolated to external data. I've owned up to a confronting perspective: I sometimes cannot even trust myself as a source. I use what I call my "uglyometer" to check whether my choices, attention and actions are informed by an ugly ego (which I attribute to fear) or being more open and spacious (which I associate with love). This clarifies my motives so I can course-correct more easily and better discern who belongs on my WATCH list.

Booster 40. What Ifs

What it's good for: Cultivating resourcefulness

What it is: This series of short, punchy, thought-provoking questions is designed to open your mind to new possibilities and perspectives.

What it does: It challenges your current thinking patterns, prompts exploration beyond your usual boundaries, and can unlock hidden potential, ultimately enhancing your motivation.

How to prepare: No preparation needed

How long it takes: 5–6 minutes

What to do: Select one or more of these questions to use as inspiration. You can pick one that immediately resonates, choose randomly, or let your intuition guide you.

Take a moment to consider what the question genuinely brings up for you right now:

1. What if what you want wants you too?
2. What if you wait too long?
3. What if today meets you where you're at?
4. What if you were to decide differently today?
5. What if you take on what's being offered?
6. What if someone else takes your place?
7. What if your vision was massive?
8. What if you choose "can" and "will" over "could" and "would"?
9. What if this is what is meant to happen?
10. What if you gave yourself full and total permission?

How it works: This booster disrupts habitual thought patterns. The "What if?" structure bypasses the brain's tendency to defend current realities and instead invites imaginative exploration. Each question is crafted to act as a mental pivot, shifting your perspective from limitations to opportunities. Some questions lean into approach motivation (for example, "What if your vision was massive?"), inspiring you toward growth, while others tap into avoidance motivation (for example, "What if you wait too long?"), encouraging action by highlighting potential missed opportunities. This blend activates different cognitive and emotional responses, broadening your sense of agency and possibility.

How to explore further: Choose a current challenge or decision you're facing and consider it through the lens of one or more of these "What if?" questions.

How it came to be: I find these questions powerfully inspiring. I particularly love the contrasting nature of how they align with either approach or avoidance motivation. They seem to offer just the right level of "kick in the pants" I need, especially when

I can't clearly see what's required. I'm continually surprised by how motivated I am by what's at stake through inaction. I would have expected the "approach" orientation to be more effective for me, but apparently that isn't always the case.

These can be truly interesting questions to raise while coaching, but they're not for everyone. For some of my clients, they incite fear rather than inspiration. Therefore, I recommend proceeding with caution, especially if you're having a wobbly day, since some of the questions may negatively impact your mental fitness in certain circumstances.

Booster 41. What It Says on the Tin

What it's good for: Cultivating resilience

What it is: This is a potent method of emotion regulation.

What it does: This booster eases suffering by soothing strong reactions and preventing or mitigating emotional hijacking. Labeling feelings offers a twofold benefit: It reduces emotion suppression (stuffing your feelings) while simultaneously redirecting energy from the limbic system, which is responsible for emotions, memory, motivation and survival behaviors, to the prefrontal cortex, where executive functions like planning, decision-making, personality expression, and moderation are managed. Moreover, it promotes emotional literacy by encouraging specificity. For example, discerning whether you're feeling livid, incensed, vexed, enraged or seething instead of broadly identifying as feeling angry. This focused effort on choosing the right word significantly aids you in calming the felt emotion.

How to prepare: No preparation needed

How long it takes: A few seconds

What to do:

1. Select one or two words that accurately describe how you're feeling in this moment. Look at the list below if you need help to find an appropriate word.
2. Speak your chosen words—under your breath, aloud at a normal volume, or shout them out. Choose the volume that best suits your current environment and maintains respect for yourself and others.
3. Remember this crucial distinction: Emotions are experienced and transient. Therefore, saying "I *feel* furious" is preferable to saying "I *am* furious."

How it works: This practice redirects the brain's limited resources (glucose and oxygen) from the limbic system to the prefrontal cortex to fuel executive functions, such as inhibition, decision-making and understanding.

How to explore further: Enhance this booster by combining it with other emotion regulation techniques offered in this book, such as "Booster 29. Reappraising Through Another Lens" on page 141, "Booster 31. Savoring the Good Stuff" on page 146, and "Booster 38. Venting Feelings" on page 159.

Renowned psychologist and researcher Paul Ekman identified seven basic emotions in his work: anger, contempt, disgust, enjoyment, fear, sadness and surprise. Later, he and his daughter, Eve Ekman, created the *Atlas of Emotions*, originally the Dalai Lama's brainchild, which further reinforces the nuanced and complex nature of being human and expands on the number of emotions we all experience.

Enjoy this glimpse into the richness of human emotion, by taking a moment to reflect on this nonexhaustive list of nouns and verbs:

acceptance	adoration	alienation
admiration	agitation	amazement

ambition
amusement
anger
anguish
annoyance
anticipation
apathy
appeasement
apprehension
appreciation
aversion
awe
awkwardness
bashfulness
belonging
bitterness
boredom
calmness
cheerfulness
clarity
compassion
confidence
confusion
contempt
contentment
courage
curiosity
cynicism
dejection
delight
depression
desire
despair
disappointment
disapproval
disbelief
discouragement
disengaged
disenchantment
discontent
disgust
dismay
distress
distrust
doubt
doubtfulness
dread
dullness
ecstasy
edginess
egotistical
elation
embarrassment
empathy
encouragement
enthusiasm
envy
euphoria
exasperation
excitement
exhaustion
fascination
fear
fervor
fluster
fondness
forlornness
forgiveness
fortitude
fragility
frustration
fury
giddiness
glee
gloom
gratefulness
gratitude
grief

guilt
happiness
hatred
heebie-jeebies
hesitation
homesickness
hope
horror
hostility
humiliation
humor
hurt
hysteria
impatience
inadequacy
incredulity
indignation
insecurity
intense
interest
intimidation
irritation
isolation
jealousy
joy
judgment
kindness
lethargy
liberation
loneliness
longing
love
malice
melancholy
mindful
mirth
modesty
mortification
nervousness
nostalgia
numbness
objection
optimism
outrage
overwhelm
panic
passion
patience
peace
perplexed
perseverance
pessimism
pity
pride
rage
regret
rejection
relief
remorse
resentment
resignation
reverence
revulsion
sadness
satisfaction
schadenfreude
scorn
security
self-doubt
self-pity
self-satisfaction
sentimentality
serendipity
serenity
sheepishness
shock
shyness
skepticism

solace
sorrow
stress
stupefaction
submission
sullen
surprise
sympathy
tedium
tenderness
terror
togetherness
triumph
trust
unease
unhappiness
vehemence
vigilance
vindication
vulnerability
warmth
weariness
weird
wistfulness
wobbly
wonder
worry
yearning
zeal

How it came to be: When I first encountered the concept of emotional literacy, I was in a relationship with someone who completely lacked it. His most frequent response to "How are you feeling?" was a sharp, dismissive "cold" or "tired," which entirely dodged my question. It was as if we were on different planets. I generally experience intense feelings coursing through me like a riptide, and if I don't regulate them, they would do my head in! For both ends of this particular spectrum, labeling can be enormously beneficial. The practice ultimately leads to improved management of oneself, of which emotion regulation is paramount.

Booster 42. WTF Model

What it's good for: Cultivating resourcefulness

What it is: Have you ever found yourself thinking "What the f***?!" in a frazzled moment? This booster transforms that universal exclamation into a playful, yet powerful, self-inquiry practice. It's intended as a structured way to hit pause and truly understand what's going on within yourself right now.

What it does: It's your personal "What the f***?!" moment, repurposed. This booster decodes your emotional, behavioral and cognitive responses—your feelings, actions and thoughts—deepening your awareness of these interconnected processes.

How to prepare: No preparation needed

How long it takes: 5–10 minutes

What to do: Using a pen and paper or a digital device, thoughtfully answer these questions:

1. How do I feel about how I'm feeling?
2. How do I feel about what I'm doing?
3. How do I feel about what I'm thinking?
4. What will I do about how I'm feeling?
5. What will I do about what I'm doing?
6. What will I do about what I'm thinking?
7. What do I think about how I'm feeling?
8. What do I think about what I'm doing?
9. What do I think about what I'm thinking?

How it works: This booster is designed to actively engage your prefrontal cortex, the part of your brain responsible for executive functions like decision-making, planning and self-regulation. By systematically asking these reflective questions, you move beyond automatic reactions and into more deliberate, conscious processing of your experiences. This introspection creates distance from overwhelming thoughts and emotions, allowing you to observe them with greater clarity and choose your responses more effectively, rather than being swept away by them.

How to explore further: There are nine questions. Are they in the optimal order for *you*? After practicing this booster a few times, consider whether any patterns have emerged that show you there's a sequence more conducive to your inquisitive mind, flow and energy. Experiment with reordering them to learn what works best.

How it came to be: This booster is based on the "How I Feel About What I'm Feeling" framework that I was introduced to by Heather Regan-Addis, cofounder of the Mindfulness Association, coauthor of the Compassion Based Living Course, and one of the brilliant tutors on the University of Aberdeen's Studies in Mindfulness program.

I need to share a completely unrelated story that still makes me laugh at my ridiculousness. At the very beginning of a thirty-hour period of silence during a retreat at Holy Isle, off the western coast of Scotland, I decided it would be a great idea to take a solo walk to the lighthouse on the other side of the island, to kick-start the process and savor my solitude in style. Minutes into it, I gently swung open the iron gate and was met by a lone seagull sitting on the grass. I politely said, "Hello," and instantly realized I'd broken my vow of silence to greet a seagull! WTF?

Chapter 11
The Mental Fitness Rocket Booster

Welcome to the Mental Fitness Rocket Booster. This is based on my 11-week program, but I wanted to make the experience more accessible, so I've offered the same core content here in a self-study format. My hope is that it gives you a structured and supportive way to work more intentionally with your mental fitness, at your own pace and in your real life. (Doing the program with me and a cohort means you are living and breathing the content as well as practicing the togetherness aspect of mental fitness. To learn more, visit mentalfitnessforhumans.com/services.)

While you can set your own schedule for the rocket booster, I advise moving through it sequentially, whether that is over the span of ten weeks, ten days, or some other cadence that works well for you. By committing to a minimum of ten days—working through one stage per day—you maximize the benefits of sleep. This pace allows your unconscious brain to process and integrate each step, a strategy I highly recommend. Each stage includes a dedicated focus, objective, outcome, practical techniques, and an optional extra boost.

Before you begin, take a few moments to set yourself up for success. (There are no right or wrong answers—you do you.)

- Consider how quickly or slowly you want to move through this rocket booster. Then, using that information, calculate a target date for completion. Does a specific date jump out at you as a potential deadline for completing your Mental Fitness Rocket Booster?
- Why is this worth doing now? What do you hope to achieve, and what does your bounce score reveal about your current mental fitness? (If you haven't already calculated your bounce score, please do so because it is a useful benchmark. Instructions can be found in "The Concept of Bounce" on page 7 if needed.)
- Which is the best medium to capture your thoughts, ideas and insights? Are you someone who loves a crisp, new journal to write in (and therefore will need to get your hands on one) or will you keep an electronic version? Regardless of your preference, how can you prepare for this experience to benefit you both now and when you wish to revisit your reflections in the future?
- When is a good time of day to dedicate to working on your mental fitness? For example, if you're doing this weekly, are you scheduling it for Saturday mornings or on Wednesday evenings? When are you most likely to be free, fresh and focused?
- Where is a good place to do this? Will you be at home, your favorite coffee shop, the beach, a forest, or on a train? Will you choose a consistent location, explore different spots, or does the exact setting not matter?
- Would you like to work through this experience in a small group so you can compare notes and directly reap the benefits of togetherness? (You can see when my next

group starts at mentalfitnessforhumans.com/services.) Or would you prefer to seize the opportunity to do some inner reflection, since solitude is more appealing to you and is aligned with your needs right now?

In the words of the beloved spiritual teacher Pema Chödrön, "The path is the goal, and the journey is how you relate to right now." To envision yours, here's a brief overview of the focus areas for each stage of the rocket booster:

- **Stage 1. Altitude:** Measuring the distance between where you are now and where you'd like to get to
- **Stage 2. Attitude:** Assessing your outlook regarding your thoughts, feelings and behavior
- **Stage 3. Aptitude:** Identifying your abilities, talents and potential
- **Stage 4. Intention:** Setting clear desired outcomes surrounding your choices and actions
- **Stage 5. Attention:** Understanding how to direct and sustain your focus effectively
- **Stage 6. Motivation:** Determining what fuels your drive and how to maintain it
- **Stage 7. Distraction:** Recognizing and reducing the pull of competing demands
- **Stage 8. Compassion:** Alleviating your discomfort
- **Stage 9. Reflection:** Evaluating your journey
- **Stage 10. Progression:** Deciding on the next steps

Finally, are there any other factors you need to consider and account for before you embark on this inner exploration?

Stage 1. Altitude

Objective: Use your bounce score to identify where you are now and decide what you want to focus on improving first, then map the distance between the two. Think of this as establishing your base camp before climbing Mt. Everest.

Outcome: Complete one of these statements: "In x days from now..." or "On x date..."

Techniques: Here are three techniques to clarify your thinking around articulating and measuring what you hope to achieve:

- Use symbolism or metaphors. Can you think of one that's suitable to represent the journey you wish to undertake and the ultimate destination? For example, imagine entering an elevator and the doors close. When they reopen, you are on a higher level.
- Break down what needs to happen or how things must change so you can achieve your aspirations.
- Imagine what it will be like to reach your goal. Go deep into this by exploring what you will be doing (behavior), how it will feel (emotions), and what you will be thinking (thoughts).

Extra Boost: Search online for visualization techniques from experts like Maya Raichoora or Mel Robbins. Alternatively, explore how you can measure outcomes in a vulnerable, honest way that moves beyond standard metrics. For example:

- That moment something goes wrong and you laugh instead of crying or getting annoyed (and you notice your improved response)
- The calm feeling of contentment you experience as you pet a beloved animal (witnessing yourself truly being in the moment)
- The sense of belonging that emerges as you consider that others are on this path too

Measurements don't have to be quantitative to be profoundly impactful. Since this is a rocket booster, your aspirations can indeed soar as high as the stars!

Stage 2. Attitude

Objective: Discover what "attitude" truly means for you by exploring your thoughts, feelings and behaviors. From this, form a clearer sense of the kind of attitude that supports your mental fitness.

Outcome: Complete this statement: "My motto for this season/year/chapter of my life is..."

Techniques: A motto is a clear, concise and memorable expression that represents your identity and aspirations, as well as your attitude. You may form one that is for you, by you, and remains private, or you may find it empowering to share it with others. Here are two techniques to clarify your thinking for this exercise:

- Harness your senses to create your motto in a novel way. For example, use your vision (select an image) or hearing (select a song or sound). This is a creative, outcome-oriented approach.
- Consider the language with which you construct your motto. For example:
  - Is it dynamic enough?
  - Does it include "will" or "can" rather than "should"? (The image of William Shakespeare holding a can of beer serves as a reminder. You're welcome!)
  - Does it encapsulate your attitude?
  - Does it complement your current bounce score?

Extra Boost: Check out Lisa Lahey and Bob Kegan's fascinating book *Immunity to Change*, in which they describe their work in underlying competing commitments. Go deeper by considering whether what you think and feel are currently in harmony or discord with what you say and do.

Stage 3. Aptitude

Objective: Explore how your unique modalities—your preferred ways of learning, processing or acting—link to your strengths and overall aptitude, recognizing your inherent ability and potential for mastering new skills through education, practice and experience, and the vast array of capabilities you possess.

Outcome: Complete this statement: "I feel most fulfilled when..."

Techniques: As Karen Armstrong, founder of the Charter for Compassion, points out in her book *Twelve Steps to a Compassionate Life*, "Human beings have always been prepared to work hard to enhance a natural ability." Here are two techniques to determine what fulfillment means to you:

- In the field of positive psychology, strengths can be broadly categorized into wisdom, courage, humanity, justice, temperance and transcendence. Try to identify one to three of your strengths in each category.
- Each day this week, check in with your mood when you wake up. You might find that what makes you feel most fulfilled when you're in a low mood is entirely different from when you're feeling lighter and more positive. On those tougher days, it's okay to give yourself a bit of a break and adjust your expectations. How else could this "mood-matching mode" fuel your mental fitness?

Extra Boost: Aptitude is strongly correlated with intrinsic motivation. Watch Dan Pink's engaging RSA Animate video,

"Drive: The surprising truth about what motivates us" for a clear introduction to the topic.

Stage 4. Intention

Objective: Set clear, context-aligned intentions as the internal driving force or gentle guide behind your choices and actions, recognizing how factors like time and life influence their effectiveness and your ability to manifest desired outcomes.

Outcome: Complete this statement: "What matters most is..."

Techniques: What intentions do you have for the week or month ahead?

- Will your intention apply at work, home or both?
- Is there any other useful context to consider?
- Check in with your mood. What would be a relevant intention for you for the rest of today?

Extra Boost: Some deeper questions to ponder:

- What do you need to let go of?
- What do you need to give yourself permission for?
- What do you want to take ownership of?
- Do your intentions fully align with what matters most?

Stage 5. Attention

Objective: Contemplate how to manage your attention—your ability to focus on specific stimuli while filtering out others—amid the countless sources vying for it, and seize the opportunity to discern what you genuinely want or need to focus on, including the influence of factors operating beneath the surface (for example, your intuition, energy levels, and immediate responses to triggers).

Outcome: Complete this statement: "It's better when I'm focused on..."

Techniques: Here are two techniques to manage and direct your attention effectively:

- Using "Booster 35. The F Model" on page 153, follow your energy to decide what to focus your attention on. Set a timer and avoid all distractions.
- Consider these reflective questions:
    - What is currently serving you in relation to what you pay attention to?
    - What might be better?

Extra Boost: You're halfway through the Mental Fitness Rocket Booster! Recheck your bounce score and compare it to the one you calculated in the preparations. This will galvanize your thoughts, feelings and ideas so far to determine what requires your continued attention.

Stage 6. Motivation

Objective: Raise your awareness of how motivation drives, directs and sustains your behavior by exploring how you use (or don't use) approach (attainment) and avoidance (prevention) motivation, and how these complementary forces can help you leverage different motivational factors.

Outcome: Complete this statement: "I am compelled to..."

Techniques: Here's one technique to try. The goal is to answer the same two questions through each of the different lenses of your trinity of self: the past you, the current you, and the future you. (It's completely up to you to decide the ages of the past and future selves you're tapping into.) The first question is about approach (your goals, desires, aims) and the second is about avoidance (what you're trying to prevent, avoid, resist). This harnesses the wisdom of your different selves by giving each a platform to offer advice, ultimately allowing you to discern whether to act upon it. Answer the following prompts:

1. My past self would advise me to prevent, avoid or resist...
2. My past self would advise me to aim toward...
3. My current self would advise me to prevent, avoid or resist...
4. My current self would advise me to aim toward...
5. My future self would advise me to prevent, avoid or resist...
6. My future self would advise me to aim toward...

Extra Boost: Some follow-up questions to contemplate:

- What patterns, if any, do you notice (for example, conflicting or similar points of view)?
- Does this exercise reinforce what compels you, or do you need more clarification around what is currently motivating you before you can complete these statements?
- Do you have a natural or learned preference for either approach or avoidance motivation, or do both resonate equally?
- Or do you find your motivation shifts depending on the context rather than following a consistent pattern?

Stage 7. Distraction

Objective: Recognize distraction as the diversion from a specific focus or intention, and rather than attempting to eliminate it, maneuver through it by making deliberate changes or taking steps to focus on what you can control—your attention, choices and actions—to achieve traction and maintain momentum despite the noise.

Outcome: Complete this statement: "In this moment, I am aware of..."

Techniques: Here are three techniques you can try to maneuver your way through distractions:

- "Booster 35. The F Model" on page 153 remains a powerful distraction-buster!
- To gain clarity and awareness about how distractions affect you, consider categorizing them. Start with fear, attention, time and energy as potential categories to understand their source. Other divisions may surface for you during this process. Also, determine whether your distractions are high-level (the forest) or detail-level (the trees) in relation to your thoughts, feelings and behavior. In other words, is this a frequent distraction across all aspects of your life, or is it related to specific stimuli? Once you've developed this awareness, are there processes you can put in place to minimize their impact? Which ones help you maintain your momentum?
- What can you continue, amend, start or stop that inhibits your engagement with whatever is attempting to distract you?

Extra Boost: Practice "Booster 13. Dynamic Mindfulness" on page 104 to bring your awareness quickly into the moment without interrupting your activity. Focus on one sense, like sight or touch, to switch from autopilot back to being present. Approach this process with nonjudgmental curiosity as your experience unfolds. After all, being easily distracted is simply part of being human!

Stage 8. Compassion

Objective: Cultivate self-compassion by recognizing it as a step beyond empathy and as a combination of understanding, willingness and desire to alleviate suffering, distinguishing between the futile goal of *ceasing* suffering and the feasible intent of *easing* it, and applying this to your experiences.

Outcome: Complete this statement: "I am managing my discomfort by..."

Techniques: Here are two techniques to try:

- What can you think about that you feel appreciative for? A conscious attempt to invoke positive feelings can offer a temporary reprieve. If you need help in this area, "Booster 29. Reappraising Through Another Lens" on page 141 is a powerful emotion regulation technique.
- What can you do to notice your experience as it unfolds and achieve equanimity in the moment? (Note: "Equanimity" isn't a frequently used word. You could swap it for "balanced," "measured" or "grounded" if you prefer, since those meanings cover the gist of it.)

Extra Boost: Try journaling about these aspects of equanimity:

- **Acceptance:** Acknowledging what is happening without needing to approve of it or wish it were different.
- **Bravery:** Having the courage to confront fear or pain through inner resolve, perseverance and connectedness.
- **Cultivation:** Continuing a proactive and ongoing process to nurture and grow by developing your ability to regulate emotion and becoming aware of your thoughts, feelings and sensations without being overwhelmed by them.

Stage 9. Reflection

Objective: Evaluate your journey on the Mental Fitness Rocket Booster in relation to your thoughts, feelings and behaviors, and recognize the opportunity to harness learning at both conscious and subconscious levels as you prepare for what comes next.

Outcome: Complete this statement: "I am learning..."

Techniques: Here's one technique to try—answer these questions and any others that may surface:

- What has changed for you during the Mental Fitness Rocket Booster? Why?
- What has persisted in your thoughts, feelings or behavior? Why?
- What change, if any, have you resisted? Why?

Extra Boost: Share your reflections with someone you trust. It's often helpful to articulate your perspective in a safe environment.

Stage 10. Progression

Objective: Harness and implement what you have gained during your experience with the Mental Fitness Rocket Booster, recognizing progression as continuous growth based on the expansion of your skills, knowledge and capabilities.

Outcome: Complete this statement: "I am pursuing..."

Techniques: Here are some techniques to determine how to continue progressing:

- Without referring to any of your earlier bounce scores, recalculate it now and only then compare it to your previous results. How might any differences inform how you continue to improve your experience?

- As you progress with your mental fitness work, ask yourself:
    - How will I prepare for the changes I want to make?
    - What do I need to do to make these shifts?
    - How will I reward myself?
    - Where can I improve my plans?
    - How can I sustain my efforts?
- These components can happen simultaneously, sequentially or in no particular order.
- Consider what these different responses represent for you.
- Identify what needs your attention as you maintain or improve your mental fitness moving forward.

Extra Boost: You did it! Congratulations on what you've accomplished, and well done for investing your time and energy into increasing your contentment and fulfillment. The extra boost this week is a virtual, collective hug of welcome from the growing group of people who are nourishing, cultivating and nurturing their mental fitness, just as you have so cleverly chosen to do.

Chapter 12
Living Better

I warmly wish you well on your mental fitness journey, and I will be imagining a world in which you increase the contentment and fulfillment in your life and work through what you've learned here.

Being human is complicated and confounding! There's absolutely no doubting that. Much of that complexity shows up in our decisions—often in ways that don't quite make sense, even to us. Mental fitness doesn't remove these challenges, but it can change how we experience them. It's a balancing act each of us performs every day.

For instance, there is a particular brand of store-bought cookie I absolutely love. It's practically perfect, except every time I wolf one down, I feel nauseous immediately after. Yet I still purchase and devour them like a true glutton for punishment. Or I get hooked on some marvel of a miniseries and break my bedtime routine in the blink of a sleepy eye. Weird behavior indeed, and even if I change these habits, I'm sure some other questionable choice will quickly take their place.

In writing this book, life didn't suddenly become easier. What changed was how it felt. My mental fitness improved—

by a lot. But I didn't change all that much, I simply became a better version of myself, warts and all. And as I organically integrated mental fitness into my professional practice, my clients reported similar shifts: the same them, only better.

That is my wish for you: not that your life miraculously transforms into an idyllic existence, but that you are better equipped to ease your suffering when it smacks you in the nose. That you are more able to regulate emotions and navigate the wonky path you tread. The aspiration is not that you try to cease suffering—there isn't a single person, higher power, or wizard who can do that—but that you become better at meeting it.

Mental fitness struck me at the right place and time on my journey and quickly emerged as both the essence of my content and fulfillment and the essential skillset for a life well-lived. In the wise words of anthropologist Wade Davis, "all of humanity is one interconnected and undivided whole." My hope is that mental fitness makes you, and those around you, feel more whole. That is how I would describe its effect on me: not perfect, not the best, not even less bonkers, just better than before.

And perhaps, as our grandchildren, great-grandchildren, and their children continue to celebrate World Mental Fitness Day (learn more at mentalfitnessforhumans.com) on April 10, they'll look back at our time and wonder how we were ever so limited in our understanding of what it means to be human. But they'll also know we were trying, and we were learning to be better!

My quest for mental fitness is a journey so grand,
With a brain that's a bit like a pile of wet sand.
When I tell myself, "Be a more competent me!"
My rebellious self will just watch some TV.

Life can be tricky, of this I've no doubt,
when one's quick to forget what one's thinking about.
In togetherness, I talk to the dog and the cat
And ponder life's meaning while lying down flat.

Some days being resourceful is one step too far,
When the voices just urge me to head to the bar.
Yet resilience grows slowly, a vine in the sun,
A quiet new strength for when hard times do come.

My wellbeing is simple, a grounded affair,
Like listening for seagulls and washing my hair.
There's comfort in moments I just let things be—
A cup of warm coffee, a lovely green tree.

So, I'll give myself grace for the stuff I don't do
And accept that my brain is a bit of a zoo.
I've learned to find kindness in matters so small
And to not be afraid when I'm destined to fall.

My spirit's unbroken, a little bit frayed,
In this life where a brave better me has been made.
As I'm here and not there, and just letting things be,
I look forward to tomorrow, for Rob Ot and me.

By Aran Dadswell, inspired by Ray Kurzweil

Thank you for reading *Better*.

If you've enjoyed reading this book, please leave a review on your favorite review site. In doing so, you can help to mainstream mental fitness and empower people to feel better about who they are and what they do.

Appendix. Cornerstone Guide

If your bounce score hints that one cornerstone could do with a little extra care, this guide will point to the boosters you can use to shore it up.

Togetherness

Meaning

Resourcefulness

Resilience

Wellbeing

Acknowledgments

I am deeply grateful to the remarkable people who contributed both directly and indirectly to this book.

My heartfelt thanks go to Will Dadswell, Yasmin Dadswell, Zoe Dobson, Jennifer Hewit, Fleur Tonner, Anna Goodwin, Julie Griffiths, Shifra Cook, Tiff Chiang, and Sara Lowe for their encouragement and belief in me.

My continued gratitude to Nelly Darmali for advising me years ago to "trust what wants to happen," which has stuck like glue ever since.

I am thoroughly inspired by the wisdom and dedicated work of so many, and my WATCH list includes Brené Brown, Shirzad Chamine, Choden, Dorie Clark, Wade Davis, Peter Diamandis, Angela Duckworth, Tasha Eurich, Elaine Fox, Barbara Fredrickson, Elizabeth Gilbert, James Gross, Rick Hanson, Arianna Huffington, Jon Kabat-Zinn, Ray Kurzweil, Willem Kuyken, Ellen Langer, Richard Layard, Lauren MacDonald, Davina McCall, Dean Mobbs, Kristin Neff, Andrew Ng, Jessica Payne, Gretchen Rubin, Sharon Salzberg, Laurie Santos, Sarah Smith, Robert Sapolsky, Tami Simon, Ruby Wax, David Wilkinson, Oprah Winfrey and John Wood.

I am deeply grateful to the marvelous Tara R. Alemany and her team at Emerald Lake Books for what they did to turn my vision into reality and deliver my book baby into this world. We learned, laughed and loved our way through this partnership—all while ensuring our own mental fitness was preserved and prioritized!

My appreciation extends to Joanna Penn, Dave Chesson, Derek Doepker, and Alexa Bigwarfe for also sharing their cleverness around "all things books."

And for providing me with an enriching sense of belonging, thank you to the inspiring communities of the Women's Mental Fitness Institute's Better Me Club, the Oxford Review, the CoachME Community, the Search Inside Yourself Leadership Institute community, British Mensa, the Kea community, ICF UK Master Certified Coach Elders, the City Women Network, and the Jigsaw Coach supervision group.

It was curious how my mental fitness blossomed when I finally shed a decades-long habit of seeking validation through unsuitable relationships. I'm lucky and grateful to belong to such a wonderful whānau (family) who have infused my life with richness and stuck with me through everything.

My breakthrough came when I embraced my fierce independence and candidly accepted my "weirdness."

This shift toward better over best carried with it a deep sense of contentment and fulfillment. It has empowered and enabled me to transition into what I like to think of as my liberated second half of this lifetime, in which I'm aspiring to be a better version of me in every moment. My ongoing intention is to be a positive source of energy and information. After all, your vibe attracts your tribe.

And with that in mind, my final, and most important, acknowledgment goes to you for choosing this book as an aid toward better mental fitness. Welcome to the tribe!

References

Adams, Fay. "Home." fayadams.com.

Armstrong, Karen. *Twelve Steps to a Compassionate Life.* The Bodley Head, 2011.

Aron, Elaine N. *The Highly Sensitive Person: How to Thrive When the World Overwhelms You*. Thorsons, 2017.

Batchelor, Martine. *Let Go: A Buddhist Guide to Breaking Free of Habits.* Wisdom Publications, 2007.

Batmanghelidj, Fereydoon. *Water: For Health, for Healing, for Life: You're Not Sick, You're Thirsty!* Balance, 2003.

Batmanghelidj, Fereydoon. "Your Body's Many Cries for Water." YouTube video by Kangen Water Australia, March 11, 2015. youtube.com/watch?v=AZVcYFZiXZE.

Baumeister, Roy F. *Meanings of Life.* Guilford Press, 1991.

Benham, Grant. "The Highly Sensitive Person: Stress and Physical Symptom Reports." *Personality and Individual Differences* 40 (2006): 1433–40. doi.org/10.1016/j.paid.2005.11.021.

Blakemore, Sarah-Jayne. *Inventing Ourselves: The Secret Life of the Teenage Brain.* Doubleday, 2018.

Bowerman, William J., and Waldo E. Harris. *Jogging.* Grosset & Dunlap, 1967.

Brach, Tara. *Radical Acceptance: Embracing Your Life with the Heart of a Buddha.* Bantam Dell, 2003.

Breus, Michael. *The Power of When: Learn the Best Time to Do Everything.* Vermilion, 2016.

Brown, Brené. *Atlas of the Heart: Mapping Meaningful Connection and the Language of Human Experience.* Vermilion, 2021.

———. *Daring Greatly: How the Courage to Be Vulnerable Transforms the Way We Live, Love, Parent and Lead.* Penguin Random House, 2015.

———. *The Gifts of Imperfection.* Hazelden Publishing, 2010.

Burgis, Luke. *Wanting: The Power of Mimetic Desire, and How to Want What You Truly Need.* St. Martin's Press, 2021.

Burkeman, Oliver. *Four Thousand Weeks: Time Management for Mortals.* Vintage, 2022.

Caltech Affect Lab. "About." Directed by Dean Mobbs. deanmobbslab.com/intro.

Chalmers, Satyam Veronica. "Home." depthorientedcoaching.com.

Chamine, Shirzad. "Take the Saboteur Assessment." positiveintelligence.com/saboteurs.

———. *Positive Intelligence.* Greenleaf Book Group, 2012.

Choden, and Heather Regan-Addis. *Compassion Based Living Course.* Mantra Books, 2025.

Chödrön, Pema. The Pema Chödrön Audio Collection. Sounds True, 2005.

———. *Start Where You Are: How to Accept Yourself and Others.* Shambhala Publications Inc., 1994.

Clear, James. *Atomic Habits: An Easy and Proven Way to Build Good Habits and Break Bad Ones.* Random House Business, 2018.

Coaching.com, "Summit." coaching.com/summit.

Coplan, Robert J. *The Joy of Solitude: How to Reconnect with Yourself in an Overconnected World*. Simon & Schuster, 2025.

Coutu, Diane. "How Resilience Works: Three Traits of Those Who Bounce Back." In *Resilience.* Harvard Business Review Press, 2017. HBR Emotional Intelligence Series.

Covey, Stephen R. *The 7 Habits of Highly Effective People: Powerful Lessons in Personal Change.* Simon & Schuster, 1989.

Cuddy, Amy. *Presence: Unlock Your Inner Confidence to Embrace Life's Biggest Challenges.* Orion Spring, 2023.

Dadswell, Aran. "The Mindfulness-to-Meaning Theory: An Exploration of How Training Related Change May Attribute to the Augmentation of Wellbeing." Dissertation, University of Aberdeen, 2018.

Das, Lama Surya. *Awakening the Buddha Within: Eight Steps to Enlightenment: Tibetan Wisdom for the Western World.* Broadway Books, 1997.

David, Iona. *Is This Love or Dopamine?* HarperCollins, 2022.

Davidson, Richard J., and Sharon Begley. *The Emotional Life of Your Brain: How to Change the Way You Think, Feel and Live.* Hodder & Stoughton, 2012.

Day, Elizabeth. *How to Fail: Everything I've Ever Learned from Things Going Wrong.* 4th Estate, 2019.

Diamandis, Peter. "Go Big, Create Wealth, Impact the World." diamandis.com.

———. "Abundance Summit 2025." March 2025.

Duckworth, Angela. *Grit: Why Passion and Resilience Are the Secrets to Success.* Vermilion, 2017.

Eastwood, Owen. *Belonging: The Ancient Code of Togetherness.* Quercus Editions Ltd, 2021.

Ekman, Paul, and Eve Ekman. "The Atlas of Emotions." paulekman.com/projects/atlas-of-emotions.

Elliott, Andrew J. "Approach and Avoidance Motivation and Achievement Goals." *Educational Psychologist* 34, no. 3 (1999): 169–89. doi.org/10.1207/s15326985ep3403_3.

Eurich, Tasha. *Shatterproof: How to Thrive in a World of Constant Chaos (and Why Resilience Isn't Enough).* Macmillan Business, 2025.

Farias, Miguel, and Catherine Wikholm. *The Buddha Pill: Can Meditation Change You?* Watkins, 2015.

Feldman, Christina, and Willem Kuyken. "Compassion in the Landscape of Suffering." In *Mindfulness: Diverse Perspectives on Its Meaning, Origins and Applications*, edited by J. Mark G. Williams and Jon Kabat-Zinn: Routledge, 2013.

Fox, Elaine. *Rainy Brain, Sunny Brain: The New Science of Optimism and Pessimism.* Arrow Books, 2013.

Fredrickson, Barbara L. *Love 2.0: Creating Happiness and Health in Moments of Connection.* Penguin Group, 2013.

Game of Thrones. "The Dragon and the Wolf." Season 7, episode 7. Directed by Jeremy Podeswa. Written by David Benioff and D. B. Weiss. Aired August 27, 2017, on HBO.

García, Héctor, and Francesc Miralles. *Ikigai: The Japanese Secret to a Long and Happy Life.* Hutchinson, 2016.

Garland, Eric L., Norman A. Farb, Philippe R. Goldin, and Barbara L. Fredrickson. "Mindfulness Broadens Awareness and Builds Eudaimonic Meaning: A Process Model of Mindful Positive

Emotion Regulation." *Psychological Inquiry* 26 (2015): 293–314. doi.org/10.1080/1047840X.2015.1064294.

Garmus, Bonnie. *Lessons in Chemistry.* Penguin Random House, 2022.

Germer, Christopher K. *The Mindful Path to Self-Compassion: Freeing Yourself from Destructive Thoughts and Emotions.* The Guilford Press, 2009.

Gilbert, Elizabeth. *Big Magic.* Bloomsbury Paperbacks, 2015.

Gilbert, Paul, and Choden. *Mindful Compassion: Using the Power of Mindfulness and Compassion to Transform Our Lives.* Robinson, 2013.

Goleman, Daniel. *Focus: The Hidden Driver of Excellence.* Bloomsbury, 2013.

Goleman, Daniel, and Richard J. Davidson. *The Science of Meditation: How to Change Your Brain, Mind and Body.* Penguin Random House, 2017.

Gordhamer, Soren. *The Essential: Discovering What Really Matters in an Age of Distraction.* Wisdom 2.0, 2025.

Gross, James J. "The Extended Process Model of Emotion Regulation: Elaborations, Applications, and Future Directions." *Psychological Inquiry* 26 (2015): 130–37. doi.org/10.1080/1047840X.2015.989751.

Hanson, Rick. *Neuro Dharma: 7 Steps to the Highest Happiness.* Rider, 2020.

Hanson, Rick, and Forrest Hanson. *Resilient: Find Your Inner Strength.* Rider, 2018.

Hassed, Craig. *Know Thyself: The Stress Release Programme.* Michelle Anderson Publishing, 2002.

His Holiness the Dalai Lama. *Beyond Religion: Ethics for a Whole World.* Houghton Mifflin Harcourt, 2011.

His Holiness the Dalai Lama, and Howard C. Cutler. *The Art of Happiness: A Handbook for Living.* Coronet, 1998.

Huffington, Arianna. "Thrive Global." thriveglobal.com.

James, William. *Talks to Teachers on Psychology: And to Students on Some of Life's Ideals.* Arc Manor, 2008.

Kabat-Zinn, Jon. *Full Catastrophe Living: How to Cope with Stress, Pain and Illness Using Mindfulness Meditation.* Bantam Books, 1990.

———. *Mindfulness for All: The Wisdom to Transform the World.* Hachette Books, 2019.

———. *Wherever You Go, There You Are: Mindfulness Meditation for Everyday Life.* Hyperion, 1994.

Kahneman, Daniel. *Thinking, Fast and Slow.* Penguin Books, 2012.

Kegan, Robert, and Lisa Laskow Lahey. *Immunity to Change: How to Overcome It and Unlock the Potential in Yourself and Your Organization.* Harvard Business Press, 2009.

Kurzweil, Ray. *The Singularity Is Nearer: When We Merge with AI.* Penguin Random House, 2024.

Langer, Ellen J. *Counter Clockwise: Mindful Health and the Power of Possibility.* Hodder & Stoughton, 2009.

———. *Mindfulness: 25th Anniversary Edition.* Da Capo Press, 2014.

Layard, Richard. "Happier Kinder Together." actionforhappiness.org.

———. *Happiness: Lessons from a New Science.* Penguin Books, 2011.

Layard, Richard, and Jan-Emmanuel De Neve. "Workplace Wellbeing." worldwellbeingmovement.org/playbook-2025.

———. *Wellbeing: Science and Policy.* Cambridge University Press, 2023.

Lee, Beth E. *The Want Mindset: The Psychology and Neuroscience of Wanting: Tap into Your Thinking to Get What You Want.* Magenta Pen Press, 2024.

Lindeblad, Björn Natthiko. *I May Be Wrong: And Other Wisdoms from Life as a Forest Monk*. Tonic, 2022.

Myss, Caroline. *Anatomy of the Spirit: The Seven Stages of Power and Healing.* Three Rivers Press, 1996.

Nairn, Rob. *Diamond Mind: A Psychology of Meditation.* Shambhala Publications, Inc., 1999.

Neff, Kristin. *Self-Compassion: Stop Beating Yourself Up and Leave Insecurity Behind.* HarperCollins, 2011.

———. "Self-Compassion." self-compassion.org.

O'Kane, Owen. *How to Be Your Own Therapist: Boost Your Mood and Reduce Your Anxiety in 10 Minutes a Day.* HQ, 2024.

Organisation for Economic Co-operation and Development. "Workplace Well-being and Progress." oecd.org/en.html.

Pavlina, Steve. "How to Discover Your Life Purpose in About 20 Minutes." January 16, 2005. mentalfitnessforhumans.com/pavlina.

Payne, Jessica. "Jessica D. Payne, PhD." jessicadpayne.com.

Penn, Joanna. *How to Write Non-Fiction: Turn Your Knowledge into Words.* Curl Up Press, 2018.

Pink, Daniel H. "Drive: The Surprising Truth About What Motivates Us." YouTube video by The RSA, April 1, 2010. mentalfitnessforhumans.com/drive.

Raichoora, Maya. *Visualise: Think, Feel, Perform Like the Top 1%.* Rider, 2025.

Ratey, John. *A User's Guide to the Brain.* Pantheon Books, 2001.

Rinpoche, Tsoknyi. *Open Heart, Open Mind: A Guide to Inner Transformation.* Rider, 2012.

Robbins, Mel. *The Let Them Theory: A Life-Changing Tool That Millions of People Can't Stop Talking About.* Hay House UK, 2024.

Rubin, Gretchen. *The Four Tendencies: The Indispensable Personality Profiles That Reveal How to Make Your Life Better (and Other People's Lives Better, Too).* Two Roads, 2017.

———. *The Happiness Project: Or, Why I Spent a Year Trying to Sing in the Morning, Clean My Closets, Fight Right, Read Aristotle, and Generally Have More Fun.* HarperCollins Publishers, 2009.

Ryan, Richard, and Edward Deci. "On Happiness and Human Potentials: A Review of Research on Hedonic and Eudaimonic Wellbeing." *Annual Review Psychology* 52 (2001): 141–66. doi.org/10.1146/annurev.psych.52.1.141.

Ryff, Carol. "Happiness Is Everything, or Is It? Exploration on the Meaning of Psychological Wellbeing." *Journal of Personality and Social Psychology* 57 (1989): 1069–81. doi.org/10.1037/0022-3514.57.6.1069.

Salzberg, Sharon. "Sharon Salzberg." sharonsalzberg.com.

———. *Real Love: The Art of Mindful Connection.* Pan Macmillan BlueBird, 2017.

Sapien Labs. "What Is Your Mental Wellbeing Score?" sapienlabs.org/mhq.

Sapolsky, Robert M. *Why Zebras Don't Get Ulcers.* W.H. Freeman, 1994.

Schwartz, Jeffrey M., and Sharon Begley. *The Mind and the Brain: Neuroplasticity and the Power of Mental Force.* HarperCollins Publishers, 2002.

Seligman, Martin. *Flourish: A New Understanding of Happiness and Wellbeing: The Practical Guide to Using Positive Psychology to Make You Happier and Healthier.* Nicholas Brealey Publishing, 2011.

Siegel, Daniel J. *Brainstorm: The Power and Purpose of the Teenage Brain.* Penguin, 2013.

Siegel, Daniel J. "Dan Siegel Hand Model." YouTube video, July 23, 2015. mentalfitnessforhumans.com/handmodel.

———. *Intraconnected: Mwe (Me + We) as the Integration of Self, Identity, and Belonging.* WW Norton & Co, 2022.

———. "Mindsight Institute." mindsightinstitute.com.

Smith, Dr. Julie. *Why Has Nobody Told Me This Before?* Michael Joseph, 2022.

Terman, Michael, and Ian McMahan. *Reset Your Inner Clock: The Drug-Free Way to Your Best-Ever Sleep, Mood, and Energy.* Penguin Group, 2012.

Thich Nhat Hanh. *Fear: Essential Wisdom for Getting through the Storm.* Harper One, 2012.

Tolle, Eckhart. *The Power of Now: A Guide to Spiritual Enlightenment.* New World Library, 1999.

Treisman, Anne M. "Strategies and Models of Selective Attention." *Psychological Review* 76, no. 3 (1969): 282–99. doi.org/10.1037/h0027242.

VIA. "VIA Institute on Character." viacharacter.org.

Walker, Matthew. *Why We Sleep: The New Science of Sleep and Dreams.* Penguin Random House, 2018.

Wax, Ruby. "Frazzled." frazzledcafe.org.

———. *A Mindfulness Guide for the Frazzled.* Penguin Random House, 2016.

———. *Sane New World: Taming the Mind.* Hodder & Stoughton, 2013.

Williams, Mark, and Danny Penman. *Mindfulness: A Practical Guide to Finding Peace in a Frantic World.* Piatkus, 2011.

Wood, John. *Leaving Microsoft to Change the World.* Collins, 2006.

———. "Room to Read." roomtoread.org.

Wood, John, and Amalia McGibbon. *Purpose, Incorporated: Turning Your Cause into Your Competitive Advantage.* Room to Read, 2017.

World Health Organization. *International Classification of Diseases, 11th Revision.* World Health Organization, 2019.

About the Author

Aran Dadswell is a mental fitness coach, speaker and founder who is endlessly curious about what it means to be human and how we might do it better.

A proud Kiwi, she has lived on four continents and worked with people from over seventy nationalities. (She keeps a list.) Her fascination with human behavior, connection and the wonderfully messy ways we navigate life has only deepened over time.

After nearly two decades in corporate roles focused on software testing and quality management, Aran shifted her attention from processes and tools to people. She holds a master of science degree in Studies in Mindfulness, a diploma in Learning and Development, and is a Master Certified Coach with the International Coaching Federation.

She is the creator of World Mental Fitness Day, observed annually on April 10, and she's already imagining how it might be celebrated decades from now and plans to still be going strong when it is.

Aran is open about the fact that her journey has been anything but linear. There have been failures, false starts, and more than a few questionable decisions along the way. What she has come to understand is that mental fitness isn't about getting it right all the time. It's about being better, not best.

She wrote this book as the resource she wishes she had years ago and as an invitation for you to explore how to navigate your journey.

Aran shares her life with her teenagers and her furry babies. The former are busy being fun, interesting, clever and very, very cool. She's hoping they'll visit frequently when she's a little old lady residing with her live-in robot, Robert Otway ("Rob Ot" for short), who will be performing all the household chores and providing daily shoulder massages. In the meantime, she continues to explore life as a work in progress—imperfect, evolving and perpetually wonky.

If you're interested in having Aran speak to your group or organization, you can contact her at emeraldlakebooks.com/dadswell.

For more great books, please visit us at
emeraldlakebooks.com.

EMERALD LAKE
BOOKS
Sherman, Connecticut

www.ingramcontent.com/pod-product-compliance
Lightning Source LLC
LaVergne TN
LVHW052312200926
848481LV00002B/539